THE BO

ONE-POT
COOKING

THE BOOK OF

ONE-POT
COOKING

MARY READER

Foreword by
BRIAN TURNER,

Photographed by
SIMON BUTCHER

HPBooks

ANOTHER BEST SELLING VOLUME FROM HPBOOKS

HPBooks
Published by The Berkley Publishing Group
200 Madison Avenue
New York, NY 10016

9 8 7 6 5 4 3 2 1

ISBN 1-55788-252-5

First United States Printing ~ August 1996

By arrangement with Salamander Books Ltd.

Food Stylist: Nicola Fowler
Printed in Belgium by Proost International Book Production

Brian Turner's recipes are featured on pages
12, 19, 28, 35, 46, 49, 58, 59, 66, 73, 75, 80, 84, 87, 88, 91, 97,
107, 115, 119.

CONTENTS

FOREWORD

'One-pot cooking' will always bring back fond memories of my days immediately after college, when I began living away from home for the first time. It was such an adventure, but not without its problems! The decisions about what to eat, when to eat and where to eat were always centered on the economics of time and money, as is so often the case today. 'One-pot cooking' provided the answer - no real cleaning up, and what a treat the last spoonfuls from the pot were!

Thirty years later, with my busy lifestyle, the need to prepare dishes that are not too time consuming is still important to me. I can prepare most of the dishes in this book in advance, freeze them if necessary, and reheat as and when I need to. What is more, the flavors mature and improve with keeping.

Cooking lots of ingredients in one pot creates dishes that merge together many different flavors. Those of us that love to cook find it so exciting to be able to experiment with dishes like these, which hardly ever fail!

Here we have a collection of dishes that brings together inventiveness, quality and the tradition of good cooking. I hope you enjoy them as much as I have.

COOKING IN ONE POT

All of the dishes in this book can be prepared using only one piece of cookware. One-pot cooking has many advantages, producing tasty, nutritious meals for people from all walks of life, from busy people with families to feed to those with limited cooking facilities. Not only convenient, it also cuts down on cleaning up and reduces fuel costs, as most of the dishes require only one source of heat.

A flameproof dish or casserole allows you to brown foods on the stovetop before transferring them to the oven.

ONE-POT RECIPES

The recipes in this book have been chosen to reflect a wide range of cooking styles and use easily available ingredients from all over the world. Many different cooking methods are used, including boiling, braising, roasting, baking or broiling, to show how versatile one-pot cooking can be.

In many of the recipes the meat and vegetables are browned or softened first on top of the stove before being cooked slowly and gently. Browning meat is not essential, but it does deepen the color of the sauce, while vegetables take on a sweeter flavor if they are sautéed in a little oil or butter first. Long gentle cooking gives the meat a special tenderness and brings out its flavor to the full, while the vegetables and other ingredients add their goodness to the juices.

Marinating is also sometimes used in the recipes. Again, this is not essential but it does add moisture to lean meats which can be rather dry, and it is also good for tenderizing tougher cuts of meat.

CHOOSING COOKWARE

Investing in good quality cookware is well worthwhile. There are so many different materials and styles available, it can be very difficult to know which one to choose, particularly if you are to rely on only one or two items.

When buying cookware it is important to be aware of the difference between flameproof and ovenproof items as some pieces of equipment can only be used with one source of heat. Because, of the techniques employed in one-pot cooking, it is best to choose cookware that is suitable for using both over direct heat and in the oven. This is more economical too, as you only need to buy one piece of equipment instead of two. Always buy the best you can afford: better materials give better cooking results and cheaper items need replacing after a short time.

FLAMEPROOF COOKWARE

Many recipes require you to start cooking on top of the stove and then continue in the oven or under the broiler. Therefore, it is essential that you choose a cooking container for this purpose that is flameproof as well as ovenproof. A dish or casserole which is only ovenproof would buckle or break if used on the stovetop.

A flameproof casserole can receive direct heat through its base. For this reason it should have a flat, stable base. If it is too thin, the food being cooked in it is apt to burn and the pan may buckle. In addition, the material used to make the pan must be able to conduct the heat evenly from the base to the rest of the pan.

The most popular choices for flameproof cookware are made of cast iron or enamel-coated cast iron. These are usually very heavy and fairly deep with straight sides. They conduct heat evenly and gently and are particularly good for dishes that require long, slow cooking. But although they give good cooking results, their weight means they are not an ideal choice for anyone who cannot lift heavy objects.

If you are looking for something lighter, then ceramic glass cookware is an excellent choice. It is both flameproof and ovenproof and can also be used under the grill.

Hard anodized aluminum pans and casseroles are also flameproof and ovenproof. They are durable, hard-wearing and completely unbreakable. Some have handles which are only suitable for using in the oven at low temperatures, but they are often adequate for casserole cooking. Others have handles made of metal and so will withstand higher temperatures. Many of these pans have a nonstick coating, which is extremely easy to clean.

Stainless steel pans with a soundly bonded aluminum base are also very good. Some have a nonstick coating, tough enough to allow you to use metal tools, and easy to clean. Always check the manufacturer's instructions before buying, to ensure that the dish can be used on the stovetop.

OVENPROOF COOKWARE

When baking or roasting, the heat conductor is the air inside the oven. This means that cookware which is only to be used in the oven does not have to be such a good conductor of heat as it does if it is used on the stovetop, so a much wider range of materials is suitable. Cast iron, copper, aluminum, ceramic glass, glass and earthenware are all efficient, but it is worth noting that metal is the best conductor of heat and it may be necessary to increase cooking times given in a recipe if you are using ceramic or glass cookware.

The size of an ovenproof dish is crucial. If it is too large, the juices or liquid in the dish could evaporate too quickly or even burn. If the dish is too small, the food may spill over the sides during cooking. Any lids should fit snugly to keep the moisture inside and prevent the food from drying out.

There is a vast range of cookware available. Choose wisely and you will need only a couple of items to produce everything from casseroles and roasts to gratins and desserts.

COOKING ON THE STOVETOP

For best results when cooking on the stovetop, place the pot over a medium heat to ensure that the outer part does not heat up too quickly, and to give good, even cooking without burning. Food could stick to the bottom if too much heat is applied too quickly. Nonstick pans should not be used over high temperatures as this may reduce the effectiveness of the coating.

• Do not allow gas flames to lick up the sides of the pan as this wastes energy - the useful heat is that applied to the base.

• Choose a burner similar in size to the base of the pan to make efficient use of the heat.

A large pan is vital for stir-frying as it allows plenty of room for turning the ingredients.

• When cooking casseroles, vegetables or pasta dishes, half-fill the pan with the cooking liquid so that it is about three-quarters full when all of the ingredients are added. This ensures that there is enough space for the food to move freely around in the liquid and to cook evenly.

• Always make sure that both the base of the pan and the cooking surface are clean and dry before use. This is particularly important when using a ceramic or halogen cooktop. Dampness can cause spitting and affect the efficiency of the cooktop. Some ceramic burners will turn themselves off if the base of the pan is too damp.

• When using a ceramic or halogen cooktop, avoid dragging the pan over the surface and be careful not to drop the pan onto the top as this could cause permanent damage.

• Try to avoid dragging a pan over a gas burner, too, as pan supports on some stoves can be a little unstable.

COOKING UNDER A BROILER

Broiling is often used as a healthier alternative to frying, but the direct heat of a broiler is also useful for browning the tops of dishes such as gratins after they have been cooked in the oven. Many stoves have the broiler in the top of the oven, so you may have to adjust the top shelf position.

• For best results, always preheat the broiler for 5 minutes before using. This enables the surface of the broiler to become evenly heated and to reach a steady temperature.

• Place the dish at least 3 inches from the elements or flame of the broiler so the heat will be even over the entire surface of the food.

COOKING IN THE OVEN

Ovens give a gentle heat, ideal for braising and casseroles.

• Preheat the oven for at least 10 minutes before use, to ensure it has reached the correct temperature and that the temperature is steady.

• Remember that ovens can vary enormously in the way they work so be prepared to adjust the temperatures given in the recipes to suit your oven.

• All cooking temperatures in the recipes are for standard ovens. If you have a convection (fan-assisted) oven, the temperature and cooking time should be reduced: consult the manufacturer's handbook for advice on your particular model.

• In standard ovens the top is always the hottest. Unless otherwise stated in a recipe, the dish should be placed on the middle shelf. In convection ovens the air is constantly circulating, so the temperature is even throughout.

COOKING IN A MICROWAVE

Although the recipes in this book give instructions for conventional ovens and stoves, many can be adapted for the microwave or partly cooked in it. A microwave can also be used for thawing and reheating frozen dishes.

• Never put metallic containers in a microwave. Some ceramic glass dishes can be transferred straight from the freezer, but be sure to check the manufacturer's handbook first.

• Remember to stir foods frequently during microwaving, to ensure they are properly heated throughout, particularly if the food has been frozen. It is vital that food reaches a high enough temperature to kill bacteria that causes food poisoning.

COOKING FOR THE FREEZER

Most of the recipes in this book are suitable for freezing. If you make larger quantities than you actually need, you can freeze the remainder for another day, saving time and energy.

• It is a good idea to freeze in small, manageable quantities, such as one or two portions, rather than large blocks. The food is not only easier to thaw this way, it allows you to be more flexible and serve varying numbers of people.

• Certain flavors may intensify when frozen, so if you are cooking specifically for the freezer you should use smaller amounts of herbs and spices. Frozen dishes containing spices, garlic and salty foods should be eaten within six weeks.

• Most foods freeze well, but avoid freezing mayonnaise (unless it is in a mousse), bananas and avocados (they discolor), whole milk and cream, although cream may be frozen if it is whipped first. Foods with a high-water content such as strawberries and lettuce become soft when thawed. Raw egg yolks or whites will freeze, but hard-cooked eggs do not freeze well.

• Make sure that you wrap foods well before freezing. Food will dry out in the freezer if the packing is not airtight. Wrapping materials should be thicker

Cookware that can be taken straight to the table for serving is always useful, so choose items that look as good in the dining room as they do in the kitchen.

than normal and strong enough not to tear easily. Containers with sealable lids are ideal for freezing, especially square ones which pack easily.

• Liquids expand on freezing, so packaging of dishes such as soups and foods with a sauce needs to allow for this. Fill the container to within 1 inch of the top and do not seal until the food is frozen.

• Always label and date the food. It is very easy to forget exactly what you have frozen after a few weeks, and some foods look very similar when they have been frozen.

• Make sure that all cooked dishes are reheated thoroughly before serving.

FROM OVEN TO TABLE

Ovenproof dishes can also be used for serving the food cooked in them, so bear this in mind when buying new cookware. Enameled cast iron, ceramic glass and earthenware can all make attractive serving dishes. Remember that the dish will be very hot when it comes out of the oven, so have a trivet on the table to prevent the pan from marking it.

BEAN & BACON SOUP

3/4 cup white haricot beans, soaked overnight
4-1/2 cups chicken stock
4 slices bacon, chopped
1 head Romaine lettuce, shredded
2 egg yolks
2/3 cup crème fraîche
1 tablespoon white wine vinegar
Salt and freshly ground pepper
Chopped fresh cilantro, to garnish

Drain beans. Rinse and drain again. Put into a Dutch oven and cover with cold water. Bring to a boil, skimming froth from surface. Drain.

Return beans to pan, add stock and bring to a boil. Add bacon and simmer 1-1/2 hours, or until beans are tender, adding more water if necessary. Remove about half beans with a slotted spoon and roughly mash them. Return to soup and stir well. Add lettuce and simmer 15 minutes.

In a bowl, mix together egg yolks, crème fraîche and vinegar. Add to soup and cook over low heat, stirring, until warmed through. Season with salt and pepper. Garnish with chopped cilantro and serve.

Makes 6 to 8 servings.

ROAST PARSNIP SOUP

1 lb. parsnips, cut into chunks
1 tablespoon olive oil
Salt and freshly ground pepper
1 large potato, cut into chunks
1 large onion, chopped
3-3/4 cups vegetable stock
2 tablespoons plain yogurt
Large pinch of freshly grated nutmeg
Plain yogurt and freshly grated nutmeg, to garnish

Arrange parsnips in bottom of a Dutch oven. Drizzle with oil and season with salt and pepper.

Cook over low heat 15 to 20 minutes, turning once, until browned all over. Add potato and onion and cook, stirring occasionally, 10 minutes. Add stock, bring to a boil, reduce heat and simmer 35 minutes.

Puree soup in a blender or food processor and return to pan. Stir in yogurt, nutmeg, salt and pepper and cook over low heat to warm through. Pour into warmed soup bowls, swirl in a little yogurt, sprinkle with nutmeg and serve.

Makes 4 to 6 servings.

— BROCCOLI & CHEESE SOUP —

8 oz. broccoli
1 tablespoon sunflower oil
1 leek, thinly sliced
6 oz. potatoes, diced
Salt and freshly ground pepper
2-1/4 cups chicken stock
2/3 cup dry white wine
1 cup (4 oz.) shredded Cheddar cheese

Cut stems from broccoli flowerets and cut into 1/2-inch pieces. Heat oil in a Dutch oven.

Add leek, potatoes and broccoli and cook, stirring occasionally, 5 minutes. Season with salt and pepper. Add stock and white wine and bring to a boil. Simmer 20 minutes, or until vegetables are tender.

Puree in a blender or food processor and return to pan. Add cheese, reserving a little for garnish, and cook over low heat, stirring, until cheese is thoroughly melted into soup. Garnish with reserved cheese and serve.

Makes 4 servings.

Note: Do not allow soup to boil after you add cheese or it will become stringy.

—BEEF & KIDNEY BEAN SOUP—

1 tablespoon olive oil
3 onions, chopped
1 lb. extra-lean ground beef
3 garlic cloves, crushed
1 teaspoon dried thyme
1 teaspoon paprika
2 teaspoons tomato paste
1 (15-oz.) can red kidney beans, drained
3-3/4 cups beef stock
1-1/4 cups tomato juice
1 teaspoon cayenne pepper
2 tablespoons chopped fresh parsley
Salt

Heat oil in a Dutch oven. Add onions and ground beef.

Cook over low heat, stirring and breaking up beef, until onions are soft and beef is browned all over. Add garlic, thyme, paprika and tomato paste. Cook over low heat 5 minutes, stirring constantly. Stir in beans, stock and tomato juice.

Bring to a boil, reduce heat, cover and simmer 10 minutes. Add cayenne and half of the parsley and season with salt. Garnish with remaining parsley and serve.

Makes 6 to 8 servings.

TUSCAN BEAN SOUP

1 tablespoon olive oil
1 bunch green onions, chopped
2 carrots, diced
2 stalks celery, sliced
2 parsnips, diced
4 oz. rutabaga, diced
4 oz. turnips, diced
2 bay leaves
4-1/2 cups chicken stock or water
2 oz. macaroni
1 (14-oz.) can cannellini beans, drained
Salt and freshly ground pepper
Chopped fresh parsley, to garnish

Heat oil in a Dutch oven. Add vegetables and bay leaves.

Cook over low heat, stirring occasionally, 10 minutes, or until soft. Add chicken stock or water and macaroni. Bring to a boil, reduce heat and simmer 25 minutes. Add beans and cook 5 minutes, to warm through.

Stir well and season with salt and pepper. Remove and discard bay leaves. Garnish with chopped parsley and serve.

Makes 6 to 8 servings.

BEET & POTATO SOUP

1 tablespoon olive oil
1 onion, chopped
8 oz. potatoes, diced
12 oz. raw beets, diced
4-1/2 cups chicken stock or water
1/2 cucumber, diced
Bouquet garni
1 tablespoon wine vinegar
1 tablespoon lemon juice
Salt and freshly ground pepper
2 tablespoons thick sour cream

Heat oil in a Dutch oven. Add onion and potatoes, and cook, stirring occasionally, 5 minutes.

Add beets, stock or water, cucumber, bouquet garni, vinegar and lemon juice. Bring to a boil, reduce heat and simmer 40 to 50 minutes.

Season with salt and pepper. Pour into warmed soup bowls, swirl in sour cream and serve.

Makes 6 to 8 servings.

FRANKFURTER SOUP

1 tablespoon olive oil
1 onion, chopped
2 slices bacon, chopped
1 small head cabbage, shredded
8 oz. carrots, sliced
1 lb. potatoes, diced
4-1/2 cups vegetable stock
12 oz. frankfurters, cut into 4 pieces
Large pinch of freshly grated nutmeg
Salt and freshly ground pepper
3 tablespoons fromage frais or sour cream

Heat oil in a Dutch oven. Add onion and bacon and cook over low heat, stirring occasionally, 5 minutes.

Add cabbage, carrots, potatoes and vegetable stock. Bring to a boil, reduce heat and simmer 15 minutes.

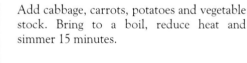

Add frankfurters and simmer 10 minutes. Season with nutmeg , salt and pepper. Stir in fromage frais and cook over low heat to warm through. Serve.

Makes 6 to 8 servings.

— FISH & MUSSEL CHOWDER —

1 tablespoon olive oil
2 slices bacon, cut into fine strips
1 large onion, finely chopped
2 potatoes, diced
2 cups chicken stock
1 lb. smoked haddock, skinned and cubed
1/2 cup all-purpose flour
20 mussels, scrubbed and trimmed
1-1/4 cups crème fraîche
Salt and freshly ground pepper
2 tablespoons chopped fresh parsley

Heat oil in a Dutch oven. Add bacon and cook, stirring, until crisp. Add onion, potatoes and stock.

Bring to a boil, reduce heat, cover and simmer 15 minutes, or until potatoes are tender. Coat haddock with flour, shaking off excess. Add to pan with mussels. Add crème fraîche and cook over low heat 3 or 4 minutes or until mussels open. Discard any mussels that remain closed.

Season with salt and pepper and stir in half of the parsley. Garnish with remaining parsley and serve.

Makes 4 to 6 servings.

-CHICKEN LIVERS WITH MANGO-

1 tablespoon olive oil
1 small onion, chopped
12 oz. chicken livers, trimmed
1-1/4 cups low-fat fromage frais or sour cream
2 teaspoons Worcestershire sauce
2 teaspoons whole-grain mustard
1 mango, sliced
Basil sprigs, to garnish

Heat oil in a flameproof casserole dish. Add onion and cook, stirring occasionally, 5 minutes, or until soft. Add chicken livers and cook, stirring, 5 minutes.

In a small bowl, mix together fromage frais or sour cream, Worcestershire sauce and mustard. Add to chicken livers in dish.

Add mango slices and cook over low heat, stirring, 2 minutes. Garnish with basil sprigs and serve immediately.

Makes 4 servings.

BAKED ZUCCHINI

4 zucchini
4oz. cooked smoked ham, chopped
6oz. goat cheese, softened
6oz. button mushrooms, finely chopped
1/4 cup walnuts, chopped
1/4 teaspoon freshly grated nutmeg
Salt and freshly ground pepper
1 cup (4oz.) shredded Emmentaler cheese
Flat-leaf parsley sprigs, to garnish

Preheat oven to 350F (180C). Cut zucchini lengthwise in half and arrange in a single layer, cut side up, in a shallow ovenproof dish.

In a bowl, mix together ham, goat cheese, mushrooms and walnuts. Stir in nutmeg and season with salt and pepper.

Spread mixture evenly over top of zucchini. Sprinkle Emmentaler cheese over top and bake 30 minutes, or until cheese is melted and golden. Garnish with flat-leaf parsley and serve.

Makes 4 servings.

—HOT CHINESE BEEF SALAD—

Finely pared zest and juice of 1 orange
1 garlic clove, crushed
1/4 cup cider vinegar
3 tablespoons hoisin sauce
1 tablespoon honey
1-1/2 lbs. beef round steak, cut into thin strips
2 teaspoons sesame oil
8 oz. chanterelle mushrooms
8 oz. fresh bean sprouts
Salt and freshly ground pepper
9 oz. mixed salad greens
Orange twists, to garnish

In a bowl, mix together orange zest and juice, garlic, cider vinegar, hoisin sauce and honey. Add beef and stir until evenly coated. Cover and refrigerate overnight. Remove beef from marinade with a slotted spoon and drain on paper towels. Heat oil in a flameproof casserole dish. Add chanterelle mushrooms and cook, stirring occasionally, 4 minutes, or until golden brown. Remove with a slotted spoon and keep warm.

Add beef, in batches, and cook, stirring, 4 minutes, or until browned and cooked through. Return all beef, mushrooms and marinade to dish and bring to a boil, stirring. Add bean sprouts, salt and pepper and cook, stirring, 2 minutes. Arrange salad greens on individual serving plates and spoon beef, vegetables and juices at side. Garnish with orange twists and serve.

Makes 4 servings.

MUSSELS IN WHITE WINE

1 tablespoon olive oil
1 small onion, finely chopped
2 plum tomatoes, peeled, seeded and chopped
Pinch of chile powder
2-1/4 cups dry white wine
3lbs. mussels, scrubbed and trimmed
Salt and freshly ground pepper
1 tablespoon chopped fresh flat-leaf parsley

Heat oil in a flameproof casserole dish. Add onion and cook over low heat, stirring occasionally, 5 minutes, or until soft. Add tomatoes, chile powder and white wine.

Bring to a boil. Add mussels, cover tightly and cook over high heat, shaking dish occasionally, 3 or 4 minutes, or until mussels open. Discard any mussels that remain closed.

Season with salt and pepper, sprinkle with parsley and serve.

Makes 4 servings.

Note: Before cooking mussels, discard any that are open and do not close when tapped sharply.

—STIR-FRIED GINGER SHRIMP—

1 tablespoon olive oil
1 red onion, sliced
1-inch piece ginger root, peeled and grated
4 oz. baby corn
1 fennel bulb, sliced
2 tablespoons lemon juice
Salt and freshly ground pepper
12 oz. cooked, peeled shrimp

Heat oil in a flameproof casserole dish. Add onion and ginger root and cook over medium heat, stirring occasionally, 3 minutes.

Add corn and fennel and cook, stirring occasionally, 4 minutes, or until vegetables are just tender.

Add lemon juice and season with salt and pepper. Add shrimp and cook, stirring, 2 minutes. Serve immediately.

Makes 4 servings.

——SCALLOPS WITH LEMON——

4 saffron strands
Juice of 1 lemon
1 tablespoon olive oil
8 sea scallops, sliced
1 bunch green onions, sliced
1 garlic clove, crushed
Salt and freshly ground pepper
2 teaspoons crème fraîche
Lemon twists, to garnish

In a small bowl, soak saffron in lemon juice 1 hour. Heat oil in a flameproof casserole dish. Add scallops and cook, stirring, 2 or 3 minutes.

Remove with a slotted spoon and keep warm. Add green onions and garlic to dish and cook over low heat, stirring occasionally, 3 minutes, or until soft. Strain lemon juice, discarding saffron strands. Add lemon juice to dish and stir well to incorporate all juices.

Season with salt and pepper. Remove from heat and stir in crème fraîche. Arrange scallops on individual serving plates and top with sauce. Garnish with lemon twists and serve.

Makes 4 servings.

Note: If scallops still have their roe attached when you buy them, you can use that in dish, too.

—WARM TROUT & NUT PÂTÉ—

1 tablespoon chopped fresh parsley
1 cup hazelnuts, chopped
12 oz. smoked trout fillets, skinned and flaked
1/4 cup fromage frais or sour cream
Salt and freshly ground pepper
Flat-leaf parsley sprigs, to garnish

Preheat oven to 350F (180C). Mix together parsley and half of the hazelnuts. Lightly oil a 3-3/4 cup ovenproof dish.

In a bowl, mix together trout, fromage frais, remaining hazelnuts, salt and pepper until well blended. Spread half of the trout mixture in dish. Sprinkle nut and parsley mixture over top. Spread remaining trout mixture on top. Smooth down to level surface.

Cover dish with a lid or piece of foil and cook in oven 20 minutes. Garnish with flat-leaf parsley and serve warm.

Makes 4 to 6 servings.

— LAYERED TURKEY TERRINE —

8 slices bacon
1 lb. ground turkey
8 oz. pork sausage
4 oz. chicken livers, trimmed and ground
1 large onion, finely chopped
1 cup fresh white bread crumbs
2 tablespoons chopped fresh basil
1/2 teaspoon salt
1/4 teaspoon freshly ground pepper
1 egg, beaten
3 tomatoes, peeled and sliced
3 oz. broccoli flowerets, chopped
Basil sprigs, to garnish

Stretch pieces of bacon by gently scraping them with back of a knife.

Use bacon slices to line bottom and side of a 3-3/4 cup ovenproof dish. Preheat oven to 350F (180C). In a bowl, mix together ground turkey, sausage, chicken livers, onion, bread crumbs, basil, salt and pepper. Stir in egg. Arrange alternate layers of turkey mixture, tomatoes and broccoli in dish, starting and finishing with turkey mixture.

Cover with a lid or foil. Place in a deep roasting pan and pour in enough boiling water to come halfway up sides of dish. Bake 2 hours, or until a skewer inserted in center comes out clean. Drain excess liquid from terrine, cover with foil and place a heavy weight on top. Refrigerate at least 2 to 3 hours, preferably overnight. Turn out terrine and cut into slices. Garnish with basil sprigs and serve.

Makes 4 to 6 servings.

—BAKED SADDLE OF SALMON—

1/4 cup butter, softened
1 garlic clove, crushed
Juice of 1/2 lemon
2 tablespoons chopped fresh parsley
1 (1-1/2-lb.) saddle of salmon, filleted
1 tablespoon olive oil
6 shallots, chopped
2/3 cup fish stock
3/4 cup red wine
1 cup veal stock
Salt and freshly ground pepper

In a small bowl, mix butter with garlic, lemon juice and 1 tablespoon of the chopped parsley.

Spread inside of one salmon piece with butter mixture and sandwich pieces back together. Wrap tightly in plastic wrap and put in freezer about 1 hour, to set. Do not freeze. Preheat oven to 400F (205C). Lightly oil a large piece of foil. Take salmon out of plastic wrap and wrap tightly in foil. Place in a shallow ovenproof dish and bake 30 to 35 minutes. Remove from dish and keep warm.

Heat oil in a flameproof dish, add shallots and cook over low heat, stirring, 3 minutes, or until soft. Add fish stock and red wine and boil until reduced and syrupy. Add veal stock and boil to reduce slightly. Add remaining parsley and season with salt and pepper. Divide sauce among warmed serving plates. Slice salmon, place on top of sauce and serve.

Makes 4 servings.

CHEESY FISH PIE

1-1/2 lbs. halibut or cod, skinned and cubed
Salt and freshly ground pepper
4 basil leaves, torn
Grated zest and juice of 1 lemon
8 oz. frozen puff pastry
1-1/4 cups plain yogurt
1 (8-oz.) can whole-kernel corn, drained
1 cup (4 oz.) shredded Emmentaler cheese
Basil sprigs, to garnish

Preheat oven to 425F (220C). Put fish in a shallow flameproof dish. Season with salt and pepper, add basil and lemon juice.

Cover with a lid or piece of foil and cook 10 to 15 minutes. Meanwhile, allow pastry to thaw 10 minutes. Add lemon zest, yogurt, corn and cheese to fish mixture and stir well. Grate pastry evenly over top.

Bake 30 to 40 minutes, or until topping is crisp and golden brown. Garnish with basil sprigs and serve.

Makes 4 to 6 servings.

CRISPY FISH HOTPOT

12 oz. zucchini, thinly sliced
2 Red Delicious apples, cored and thinly sliced
1 large onion, sliced
6 oz. small green beans, cut into 1-inch lengths
1 teaspoon dried sage
1-1/4 cups fish stock
1-1/2 lbs. cod fillet, skinned and cubed
Salt and freshly ground pepper
12 oz. potatoes with skins on, thinly sliced
3/4 cup (3 oz.) shredded Cheddar cheese

Preheat oven to 375F (190C). Arrange layers of zucchini, apples, onion and beans in an ovenproof casserole dish.

Sprinkle with sage and pour in stock. Cover and bake 30 minutes. Remove from oven, arrange fish on top and season with salt and pepper.

Arrange sliced potatoes on top, sprinkle with cheese and bake 35 to 40 minutes, or until potatoes are tender and cheese is melted and golden. Serve hot.

Makes 4 to 6 servings.

Variation: Any firm white fish fillets, such as whiting or haddock, can be used instead of cod in this recipe.

KEDGEREE

1 lb. smoked haddock
2 tablespoons olive oil
1 onion, chopped
1-1/2 cups easy-cook rice
4 hard-cooked eggs, shelled
2 tablespoons crème fraîche
2 tablespoons butter
3 tablespoons chopped fresh parsley
Salt and freshly ground pepper

Put haddock in a flameproof casserole dish with 3-3/4 cups water. Bring to a boil, reduce heat and simmer 10 minutes, or until fish is tender. Remove haddock with a slotted spoon and keep warm.

Pour cooking liquid from dish and set aside. Heat oil in pot, add onion and cook, stirring occasionally, 5 minutes, or until soft. Add rice and cook, stirring, 1 minute. Pour reserved cooking liquid over rice, bring to a boil, reduce heat, cover and simmer 15 to 20 minutes, or until liquid has been absorbed and rice is tender. Remove from heat.

Cut hard-cooked eggs into wedges. Flake haddock and gently mix into rice with eggs, crème fraîche, butter and parsley. Season with salt and pepper. Return to heat and cook over low heat 2 or 3 minutes, to warm through.

Makes 4 servings.

SEAFOOD RISOTTO

1 tablespoon olive oil
6 green onions, chopped
1 garlic clove, crushed
1 cup Arborio rice
1/2 teaspoon turmeric
2-1/4 cups fish stock
1/4 cup dry white wine
4 tomatoes, chopped
1 lb. mixed cooked seafood
12 raw jumbo shrimp
6 oz. frozen green peas
Salt and freshly ground pepper
1/4 cup chopped fresh parsley

Heat oil in a flameproof casserole dish. Add green onions and garlic and cook, stirring, 3 minutes, or until soft. Cover and cook over low heat 2 minutes. Add rice and turmeric and cook, stirring, 1 minute. Add half of the stock, the wine and tomatoes to dish. Bring to a boil, reduce heat, cover and simmer 10 minutes.

Add remaining stock, bring back to a boil, reduce heat, cover and cook 15 minutes, or until rice has absorbed most of liquid. Stir in seafood, shrimp, peas, salt and pepper. Cook over low heat, stirring occasionally, 10 minutes. Stir in parsley and serve.

Makes 4 servings.

- MACKEREL WITH SOUR CREAM -

4 (4-oz.) mackerel or other fish fillets, skinned
1 leek, thinly sliced
1 (7-oz.) can crushed tomatoes
1 tablespoon chopped fresh dill
1/2 teaspoon mild paprika
Juice of 1/2 lemon
Salt
2/3 cup thick sour cream
Dill sprigs, to garnish

Preheat oven to 400F (205C). Place fish in a shallow ovenproof dish.

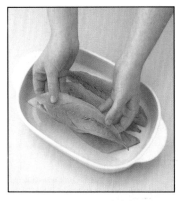

In a large bowl, mix together leek, tomatoes, dill, paprika and lemon juice and pour over mackerel. Season with salt.

Cover with a lid or piece of foil and bake 50 minutes, or until fish is cooked through. Drizzle sour cream over fish, garnish with dill sprigs and serve.

Makes 4 servings.

Note: To prepare leeks, cut off dark green tops and root ends. Slice white part almost in half lengthwise, then rinse under cold running water to remove sand.

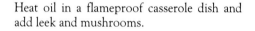

SEAFOOD LASAGNE

2 tablespoons olive oil
1 leek, thinly sliced
8oz. mushrooms, thinly sliced
8oz. haddock fillet, skinned and cubed
4oz. cooked, peeled shrimp
10oz. cod fillet, skinned and cubed
2 tablespoons lemon juice
Salt and freshly ground pepper
4 eggs, beaten
1/2 cup freshly grated Parmesan cheese
2-1/4 cups plain yogurt
6 wide fresh lasagne noodles
8oz. mozzarella cheese, sliced

Heat oil in a flameproof casserole dish and add leek and mushrooms.

Cook over low heat 10 minutes, stirring occasionally, until soft. Add haddock, shrimp, cod, lemon juice, salt and pepper and cook, stirring, 5 minutes. Preheat oven to 350F (180C). Mix together eggs, Parmesan cheese and yogurt. Stir two-thirds of egg mixture into fish mixture. Remove two-thirds of fish mixture from dish.

Cover fish mixture in dish with 2 lasagne noodles. Cover them with half of remaining fish mixture, then 2 more lasagne noodles. Spread remaining fish mixture over noodles. Cover with remaining noodles and pour reserved egg mixture over top. Cover with cheese and bake 40 to 50 minutes, or until topping is golden and pasta is tender. Serve.

Makes 6 to 8 servings.

——— HADDOCK & SALMON PIE ———

1/4 cup butter
1/2 cup all-purpose flour
1-1/4 cups milk
1-1/4 cups fish stock
12 shallots
1 lb. potatoes, diced
2 garlic cloves, crushed
2 tablespoons olive oil
1 tablespoon whipping cream
Salt and freshly ground pepper
2 tablespoons whole-grain mustard
1/4 cup chopped fresh parsley
1 lb. salmon fillet, skinned and cubed
8 oz. smoked haddock, skinned and cubed
12 small button mushrooms
1 egg, beaten

Melt butter in a flameproof casserole dish, add flour and cook over low heat, stirring, 2 minutes. Gradually stir in milk and fish stock, then add shallots. Bring to a boil, reduce heat and simmer 30 minutes. Meanwhile, cook potatoes and garlic in boiling salted water 20 minutes, or until potatoes are tender. Drain. Mash potatoes and garlic and stir in olive oil, cream, salt and pepper. Set aside. Preheat oven to 400F (205C).

Season shallot sauce with salt and pepper and add mustard and parsley. Add salmon, haddock and button mushrooms and simmer 10 minutes. Pipe or spoon potato on top of fish mixture and bake 10 minutes. Take out of oven and brush with a little beaten egg. Return to oven and bake 20 minutes, or until potato is golden.

Makes 4 to 6 servings.

—— HALIBUT WITH ORANGE ——

1/2 cup all-purpose flour
1/2 teaspoon freshly grated nutmeg
4 (6-oz.) halibut steaks
2 tablespoons butter
6 green onions, sliced
3/4 cup fresh orange juice
1 tablespoon Worcestershire sauce
Juice of 1/2 lemon
Salt and freshly ground pepper

Mix together flour and nutmeg and use to coat halibut.

Heat butter in a shallow flameproof casserole dish. Add green onions and cook, stirring occasionally, 3 minutes, or until soft. Add halibut and cook over low heat 5 or 6 minutes on each side until just cooked. Remove from dish with a fish slice and keep warm.

Add orange juice, Worcestershire sauce, lemon juice, salt and pepper to dish and boil rapidly until reduced and thickened. Pour over fish and serve.

Makes 4 servings.

──PASTA WITH TUNA SAUCE──

8 oz. pasta twists
1 (7-oz.) can tuna in water, drained
1 (8-oz.) can whole-kernel corn, drained
1 green bell pepper, diced
4 green onions, cut into 1-inch lengths
1 (10-oz.) can condensed mushroom soup mixed
    with 1/2 can water
Salt and freshly ground pepper
Flat-leaf parsley sprigs, to garnish

Add pasta twists to a large pot of boiling salted water and cook 10 minutes, or according to package instructions, until almost tender.

Drain pasta and return to pot. Add tuna, corn, bell pepper and green onions and stir to combine.

Stir soup into pasta. Cook over low heat, stirring occasionally, 20 minutes. Season with salt and pepper. Garnish with flat-leaf parsley and serve.

Makes 4 servings.

── TUNA-STUFFED PEPPERS ──

4 large green bell peppers
3/4 cup long grain rice, cooked
1 (7-oz.) can tuna in water, drained and flaked
1 small onion, grated
1 (8-oz.) can whole-kernel corn, drained
2 oz. mushrooms, finely chopped
1 teaspoon paprika
Salt and freshly ground pepper
1/2 cup (2 oz.) shredded Cheddar cheese
4 slices tomato

Trim bottom of each bell pepper so it will stand. Combine rice, tuna, onion, corn, mushrooms, paprika, salt and pepper in a large bowl. Pack into bell peppers.

Preheat oven to 350F (180C). Place bell peppers in a shallow ovenproof dish. Pour 3-3/4 cups water into dish and bake 30 minutes.

Remove from oven and increase temperature to 400F (205C). Sprinkle bell peppers with cheese. Top each one with a slice of tomato and return to oven 10 minutes. Serve hot.

Makes 4 servings.

PASTA WITH TROUT

1 tablespoon olive oil
8 oz. pink-fleshed trout fillets, skinned and cubed
8 oz. small broccoli flowerets
10 oz. tagliatelle
2/3 cup half-and-half
1 tablespoon chopped fresh dill
Salt and freshly ground pepper
1/4 cup toasted flaked almonds

Heat oil in a flameproof casserole dish. Add trout and broccoli and cook, stirring occasionally, 10 to 15 minutes, or until fish is just cooked and broccoli is tender.

Meanwhile, cook tagliatelle in boiling salted water 8 to 10 minutes, or according to package instructions, until just tender. Drain and stir in to dish.

Stir in half-and-half and dill and season with salt and pepper. Sprinkle with toasted almonds and serve.

Makes 4 servings.

——CANTONESE SHRIMP——

1 tablespoon olive oil
1 onion, sliced
2 teaspoons five-spice powder
1 lb. cooked, peeled jumbo shrimp
1 red bell pepper, sliced
1 (8-oz.) can sliced water chestnuts, drained
6 oz. snow peas
Flat-leaf parsley, to garnish

Heat oil in a flameproof casserole dish. Add onion and cook, stirring occasionally, 5 minutes, or until soft. Add five-spice powder and cook, stirring, 1 minute. Add shrimp and cook 2 or 3 minutes.

Stir in bell pepper, water chestnuts and snow peas. Cover and cook 2 or 3 minutes. Garnish with flat-leaf parsley and serve.

Makes 2 or 3 servings.

——SMOKED FISH GRATIN——

1 lb. peppered smoked mackerel or other fish,
   skinned and flaked
1/4 cup chopped fresh parsley
2-1/4 cups fromage frais or plain yogurt
2 tablespoons prepared horseradish
6 to 8 drops hot pepper sauce
1 red onion, finely chopped
2 tablespoons grated Parmesan cheese
3 cups fresh whole-wheat bread crumbs
1 oz. sunflower kernels

Preheat oven to 400F (205C). Mix together
fish, parsley, fromage frais or plain yogurt,
horseradish, hot pepper sauce and onion.

Spread fish mixture into a shallow ovenproof
dish. Mix together Parmesan cheese, bread
crumbs and sunflower kernels.

Scatter over fish mixture and bake 20
minutes, or until golden. Serve hot.

Makes 4 to 6 servings.

– COD & VEGETABLE PACKAGES –

4 cod steaks, each weighing 6 oz.
8 oz. frozen mixed vegetables
6 green onions, sliced
2 tablespoons sweet sherry
2 teaspoons soy sauce
1/2-inch piece ginger root, peeled and thinly sliced
Lemon slices, to serve

Preheat oven to 400F (205C). Cut four large squares of foil and lightly oil. Place a cod steak on each one. Arrange frozen vegetables and green onions on top.

Mix together sherry and soy sauce and spoon over cod steaks. Put sliced ginger on top.

Bring foil up over steaks and fold edges together to seal. Put packages in an ovenproof dish and bake 20 to 25 minutes. Remove fish and vegetables from foil and serve with lemon slices.

Makes 4 servings.

— TROUT WITH VEGETABLES —

2 (14-oz.) cans crushed tomatoes
1 leek, finely sliced
12 basil leaves, torn
2 teaspoons chopped fresh oregano
3 stalks celery, diced
2 zucchini, diced
3/4 cup red wine
2 tablespoons red wine vinegar
Salt and freshly ground pepper
4 trout, ready to cook
4 basil sprigs
8 oregano sprigs

Put tomatoes, leek, torn basil, chopped oregano, celery, zucchini, wine and vinegar in a shallow flameproof casserole dish.

Bring to a boil, reduce heat, cover with a lid or piece of foil and simmer 10 minutes. Season with salt and pepper. Stuff trout cavities with basil sprigs and half of the oregano sprigs.

Place trout on top of vegetable mixture. Cover again and simmer 20 to 25 minutes, or until trout is cooked through. Garnish with remaining oregano sprigs and serve.

Makes 4 servings.

- STUFFED CORNISH GAME HENS -

4 Cornish game hens
Watercress sprigs, to garnish
STUFFING:
2 cups fresh whole-wheat bread crumbs
2oz. dried apricots, chopped
1 small bunch watercress, chopped
1/2 cup hazelnuts, chopped
Salt and freshly ground pepper
1 egg yolk
WATERCRESS SAUCE:
1 onion, finely chopped
1 bunch watercress, chopped
1/2 cup dry white wine
1 tablespoon chopped fresh tarragon
1 teaspoon lemon juice
1/4 cup plain yogurt

Preheat oven to 400F (205C). To make stuffing, mix together bread crumbs, apricots, watercress, hazelnuts, salt and pepper. Stir in egg yolk. Use to stuff cavity of each hen. Place hens in a shallow flameproof dish and roast 50 to 60 minutes, or until cooked through. To test, pierce thigh with a skewer: if juices run clear hens are cooked. Remove hens from dish and keep warm.

To make watercress sauce, add onion to cooking juices in dish and cook over low heat, stirring occasionally, 5 minutes, or until soft. Add chopped watercress and stir well. Add white wine, tarragon and lemon juice and heat gently. Stir in yogurt and season with salt and pepper. Heat gently to warm through. Pour sauce on to warmed serving plates and place hens on top. Garnish with watercress and serve.

Makes 4 servings.

— CHILE CHICKEN WITH RICE —

1 chicken, quartered
Salt and freshly ground pepper
2/3 cup chicken stock
2/3 cup dry white wine
1 teaspoon hot chile sauce
1 cup Basmati rice
1 onion, chopped
1 yellow bell pepper, chopped
1 fresh green chile, seeded and chopped
1 (14-oz.) can crushed tomatoes
Flat-leaf parsley sprigs, to garnish

Preheat oven to 425F (220C). Place chicken in a large casserole dish. Season with salt and pepper.

Bake 20 minutes. Remove chicken from dish and keep warm. Reduce oven temperature to 375F (190C). Add stock, white wine, chile sauce and 1/2 cup boiling water to dish. Add rice, onion and bell pepper. Stir in chopped green chile and tomatoes.

Place chicken on top of rice mixture. Cover and bake 45 minutes, or until rice is tender and liquid has been absorbed. Garnish with flat-leaf parsley and serve.

Makes 4 servings.

SPICY CHICKEN

2 garlic cloves, crushed
1/2-inch piece ginger root, peeled and very thinly sliced
1 tablespoon soy sauce
1/2 teaspoon five-spice powder
1 (3-lb.) chicken, cut into 8 pieces
2 tablespoons olive oil
2 onions, thinly sliced
1 red bell pepper, thinly sliced
8 plum tomatoes, peeled, quartered and seeded
2 tablespoons chopped fresh cilantro

In a large bowl, mix together garlic, ginger root, soy sauce and five-spice powder. Add chicken and turn to coat.

Cover and marinate 2 hours. Preheat oven to 350F (180C). Heat oil in a large flameproof casserole dish. Add onions and bell pepper, cover and cook over low heat 10 to 15 minutes, or until soft but not colored. Add tomatoes.

Add chicken and marinade, cover and bake 25 to 30 minutes, or until chicken is cooked through. Sprinkle with cilantro and serve.

Makes 4 servings.

CHICKEN CRUMBLE

1 tablespoon olive oil
1 lb. skinless, boneless chicken breasts, cubed
1 leek, sliced
8 oz. mushrooms, thinly sliced
4 oz. frozen green peas
2 cups plain yogurt
2 teaspoons whole-grain mustard
Salt and freshly ground pepper
2/3 cup rolled oats
1/2 cup whole-wheat flour
1/4 cup butter
1 cup fresh whole-wheat bread crumbs
1 tablespoon grated Parmesan cheese
2 teaspoons dried thyme
1 tablespoon sesame seeds
Thyme sprigs, to garnish

Heat oil in a large flameproof casserole dish. Add chicken and cook, stirring, until golden on all sides. Add leek and cook, stirring occasionally, 10 minutes, or until leek is soft. Preheat oven to 400F (205C). Add mushrooms and peas to dish and cook 3 to 5 minutes, or until peas have thawed. Remove from heat and stir in yogurt, mustard, salt and pepper.

Put oats and flour in a bowl and cut in butter until mixture resembles bread crumbs. Stir in bread crumbs, Parmesan cheese, thyme and sesame seeds. Sprinkle mixture evenly over top of chicken and bake 40 to 45 minutes, or until topping is golden brown. Garnish with thyme sprigs and serve.

Makes 4 servings.

— GARLIC ROASTED CHICKEN —

2 tablespoons olive oil
6 garlic cloves, thinly sliced
8 chicken thighs
4oz. fennel, cut into wide strips
1 carrot, cut into wide strips
1 parsnip, cut into wide strips
1 large potato, diced
1 red bell pepper, diced
1 green bell pepper, diced

Preheat oven to 425F (220C). Heat oil in a shallow flameproof dish. Add garlic and cook 2 or 3 minutes. Add chicken and vegetables and turn to coat.

Bake 55 or 60 minutes, or until juices are clear when chicken is pierced with a fork. Serve hot.

Makes 4 servings.

— FLEMISH BRAISED CHICKEN —

1/4 cup butter
1 (4-lb.) chicken
1 lb. leeks, sliced
8 oz. carrots, sliced
1/2 head celery, chopped
4 oz. button mushrooms, halved
2-1/2 cups chicken stock
2 bay leaves
12 small new potatoes
1 cup dry white wine
1/3 cup whipping cream
2 egg yolks
Flat-leaf parsley sprigs and chopped parsley, to garnish

Melt butter in a large flameproof casserole dish. Add chicken and brown all over.

Remove from dish. Preheat oven to 400F (205C). Add leeks, carrots, celery and mushrooms to dish and stir well. Cover and cook 5 to 10 minutes, or until soft. Add stock and bay leaves. Bring to a boil and add chicken. Cover and bake 30 minutes. Add potatoes and cook 30 minutes. Lift out chicken and remove vegetables with a slotted spoon. Keep warm.

Add wine to dish and bring to a boil. Reduce to a simmer. In a large bowl, mix together cream and egg yolks. Pour some hot stock into cream mixture, stirring constantly. Return to dish and heat through. Do not boil. Return vegetables to dish. Carve chicken, garnish with parsley sprigs and chopped parsley and serve with vegetables and sauce.

Makes 6 servings.

THAI CHICKEN

2 teaspoons olive oil
1 fresh red chile, seeded and finely chopped
1-inch piece ginger root, peeled and grated
1 teaspoon lemon grass paste
8 oz. chanterelle mushrooms
1 or 2 teaspoons Thai red curry paste
1 cup coconut milk
1 tablespoon light soy sauce
12 oz. skinless, boneless chicken breasts, cubed
Cilantro sprigs and chopped cilantro, to garnish

Heat oil in a flameproof casserole dish. Add chile, ginger root, lemon grass paste and mushrooms and stir-fry 2 or 3 minutes.

Add curry paste and stir-fry 1 minute. Add coconut milk and soy sauce and bring to a boil.

Add chicken and simmer 10 minutes, or until chicken is tender and cooked through. Garnish with cilantro sprigs and chopped cilantro and serve.

Makes 4 servings.

Note: If lemon grass paste is not available, replace it with 1 teaspoon chopped fresh lemon grass, or 1/2 teaspoon dried.

STIR-FRIED DUCK

4 (about 4-oz.) boneless duck breasts
2 tablespoons vegetable oil
1 garlic clove, crushed
1-inch piece ginger root, peeled and grated
1/4 cup soy sauce
2 carrots, cut into matchsticks
8 oz. snow peas
3 stalks celery, cut into matchsticks
10 oz. fresh bean sprouts
1 teaspoon cornstarch

Remove skin and excess fat from duck breasts and cut flesh into strips.

Heat oil and garlic in a large flameproof casserole dish. Add duck, ginger root and soy sauce and stir-fry 3 or 4 minutes. Add carrots, snow peas and celery and stir-fry 5 minutes. Add bean sprouts and stir-fry 1 minute.

Blend cornstarch with 2 tablespoons and add to dish. Cook, stirring, 1 or 2 minutes, or until juices have thickened. Serve.

Makes 4 servings.

- DUCK WITH APPLES & PRUNES -

1 tablespoon olive oil
4 (about 4-oz.) duck breasts
2 cooking apples, peeled and sliced
8 oz. pitted prunes
2-1/2 cups unsweetened apple juice
Salt and freshly ground pepper

Preheat oven to 400F (205C). Heat oil in a shallow flameproof casserole dish, add duck and cook 3 or 4 minutes on each side, until browned.

Cover with apple slices and prunes. Pour apple juice over duck and season with salt and pepper. Bring to a boil, cover with a lid or piece of foil and bake 55 or 60 minutes, or until duck is cooked through. Remove duck from dish with a slotted spoon, leaving behind apples and prunes, and keep warm.

Bring cooking juices in dish to a boil and boil 5 minutes, or until liquid has reduced and thickened. Pour sauce, apples and prunes over duck and serve.

Makes 4 servings.

GREEK MEATBALLS

1 lb. ground turkey
1 onion, finely chopped
1 garlic clove, crushed
1 tablespoon chopped fresh parsley
1 tablespoon chopped fresh mint
3 eggs, separated
1/2 cup cooked rice
Salt and freshly ground pepper
4-1/2 cups chicken stock
Juice of 1 lemon
1 (8-oz.) package frozen green peas
Mint sprigs, to garnish

Mix together turkey, onion, garlic, herbs, egg yolks, rice, salt and pepper. Divide mixture into 24 balls.

Leave mixture to rest 20 minutes. Place meatballs in a single layer in a large flameproof casserole dish. Cover with chicken stock. Bring to a boil, reduce heat and simmer 20 minutes, turning regularly to ensure even cooking. Remove meatballs with a slotted spoon and keep warm. Boil stock until reduced by two-thirds.

Beat egg whites with lemon juice until frothy. Add to hot stock in dish. Stir in peas and return meatballs to dish. Heat gently to warm through. Garnish with mint sprigs and serve.

Makes 4 servings.

TURKEY KORMA

1 teaspoon turmeric
1 teaspoon ground cumin
1 teaspoon ground coriander
1/2 teaspoon ground ginger
2/3 cup plain yogurt
2 teaspoons lemon juice
1/2 cup coconut milk
1/2 cup chicken stock
3 oz. unsweetened shredded coconut
Salt and freshly ground pepper
1 lb. cooked turkey meat, cubed
Cilantro sprigs, to garnish

Preheat oven to 375F (190C). Dry-fry turmeric, cumin, coriander and ginger in a flameproof casserole dish 2 or 3 minutes.

Add yogurt, lemon juice, coconut milk, stock, shredded coconut, salt and pepper and mix well. Stir in turkey.

Bring to a boil, cover and bake 30 to 40 minutes. Garnish with cilantro sprigs and serve.

Makes 4 servings.

— GINGER TURKEY & CABBAGE —

1-1/4 cups red wine
2 tablespoons red wine vinegar
2/3 cup raisins
8oz. dried apricots, halved
1-inch piece ginger root, peeled and grated
2 garlic cloves, crushed
Salt and freshly ground pepper
4 turkey breast fillets, each weighing 6 oz.
1/2 head red cabbage, shredded
Flat-leaf parsley sprigs, to garnish

In a large bowl, mix together red wine, vinegar, raisins, apricots, ginger root, garlic, salt and pepper. Add turkey.

Cover and marinate in the refrigerator at least 2 hours or overnight. Preheat oven to 400F (205C). Arrange red cabbage in a shallow ovenproof dish. Remove turkey from marinade and mix marinade with cabbage. Place turkey on top.

Bake 45 to 50 minutes, or until turkey is tender and cooked through. Garnish with flat-leaf parsley and serve.

Makes 4 servings.

TURKEY MILANESE

1 egg, beaten
2 cups fresh white bread crumbs
Grated zest and juice of 1 lemon
Salt and freshly ground pepper
4 turkey breast fillets, each weighing 4 oz., pounded
   until thin
2 tablespoons butter
2 tablespoons olive oil
12 oz. zucchini, sliced
2 teaspoons chopped fresh tarragon
Lemon wedges, to serve

Place egg in a shallow bowl. Mix together bread crumbs, lemon zest, salt and pepper and put on a large plate. Dip turkey in egg and then bread crumbs.

Preheat oven to 400F (205C). Heat butter and oil in a shallow flameproof casserole dish. Add turkey and cook 3 minutes on each side, until crisp and golden. Add zucchini and tarragon.

Sprinkle with lemon juice and season with pepper. Cover and bake 35 to 40 minutes. Serve with lemon wedges.

Makes 4 servings.

— TURKEY WITH CHESTNUTS —

4 turkey breast fillets, each weighing 6 oz.
4 slices bacon, chopped
2 tablespoons olive oil
2 tablespoons chopped fresh parsley
1 teaspoon sugar
1 tablespoon balsamic vinegar
Freshly ground pepper
1 (8-1/2-oz.) can chestnuts, coarsely chopped
4 oz. cherry tomatoes, halved
Flat-leaf parsley sprigs, to garnish

Put turkey in a shallow flameproof casserole dish and scatter bacon on top. Cook over medium heat 15 minutes, turning once, until golden and cooked through.

Remove turkey and bacon with a slotted spoon and keep warm. In a bowl, whisk together olive oil, parsley, sugar, balsamic vinegar and pepper. Stir in chestnuts and cherry tomatoes.

Stir chestnut mixture into cooking juices in dish and cook, stirring, 2 minutes. Divide relish among warmed serving plates and place turkey breasts and bacon on top. Garnish with flat-leaf parsley and serve.

Makes 4 servings.

–PHEASANT IN PARSLEY SAUCE–

1/4 cup butter
2 pheasants, ready to cook
1 bunch fresh parsley
3 onions, thinly sliced
1/4 cup all-purpose flour
1-1/4 cups chicken stock
2/3 cup crème fraîche
Salt and freshly ground pepper
Flat-leaf parsley sprigs, to garnish

Preheat oven to 350F (180C). Melt butter in a large flameproof casserole dish. Add pheasants and cook until browned all over. Remove and keep warm.

Separate thick parsley stalks from leaves and tie stalks together with string. Chop leaves and set aside. Add onions to dish and cook, stirring occasionally, 7 minutes, or until soft and lightly colored. Add flour and cook, stirring, 1 minute. Gradually add chicken stock, stirring constantly until smooth. Bring to a boil and add bundle of parsley stalks. Add pheasants, cover and bake 1 hour or until tender.

Remove pheasants from dish and keep warm. Remove and discard parsley stalks. Add chopped parsley and crème fraîche to sauce and season with salt and pepper. Heat gently to warm through. Cut pheasants in half with kitchen scissors. Garnish with flat-leaf parsley sprigs and serve with parsley sauce.

Makes 4 servings.

—RABBIT IN MUSTARD SAUCE—

1/4 cup butter
8 rabbit pieces
1 cup dry white wine
1/2 cup Dijon mustard
1 thyme sprig
Salt and freshly ground pepper
1/2 cup plain yogurt
Chopped fresh flat-leaf parsley and thyme sprigs, to
    garnish

Melt butter in a flameproof casserole dish. Add rabbit and cook 5 to 10 minutes, turning, until browned all over. Remove with a slotted spoon.

Stir in wine, mustard, thyme, salt and pepper and bring to a boil. Return rabbit to dish, cover and simmer 25 minutes or until tender. Remove rabbit with a slotted spoon and keep warm.

Boil sauce until reduced by half. Remove and discard thyme sprig and stir in yogurt. Warm through over low heat. Garnish rabbit with chopped parsley and thyme sprigs, add sauce and serve.

Makes 4 servings.

—QUAIL IN A MASALA SAUCE—

8 quails
1 tablespoon melted butter
Mint sprigs and salad greens, to garnish
MARINADE:
1-1/4 cups plain yogurt
1 small onion, finely chopped
1 tablespoon finely chopped fresh mint leaves
1 tablespoon finely chopped cilantro leaves
1 garlic clove, crushed
1-inch piece ginger root, peeled and grated
1 tablespoon garam masala
Juice of 1 lemon
1 teaspoon salt

Put quails in a large dish. Mix together marinade ingredients and pour over quails.

Cover and marinate in the refrigerator at least 2 hours, preferably overnight. Preheat oven to 425F (220C). Remove quails from marinade, reserving marinade. Thread quails on to skewers and sit skewers over an ovenproof dish.

Bake 40 minutes, basting with melted butter, until quails are tender. Remove quails and keep warm. Add reserved marinade to dish and stir to combine with cooking juices. Bring to a boil, stirring. Garnish quails with mint sprigs and salad greens and serve with masala sauce.

Makes 4 servings.

ROASTED GUINEA FOWL

1 tablespoon olive oil
2 guinea fowl
4 slices bacon, chopped
6 oz. button mushrooms
6 oz. shallots
2 tablespoons brandy
1 cup red wine
2-1/2 cups chicken stock
3 tablespoons red currant jelly
Salt and freshly ground pepper
Marjoram sprigs, to garnish

Preheat oven to 350F (180C). Heat oil in a flameproof casserole dish. Add guinea fowl and brown all over.

Cover and bake 35 to 40 minutes or until tender. Remove and keep warm. Add bacon, mushrooms and shallots to dish and cook, stirring, 4 or 5 minutes, or until golden brown. Remove with a slotted spoon and keep warm. Add brandy, wine, stock and red currant jelly to cooking juices and stir well. Bring to a boil, stirring, and boil 20 to 25 minutes, stirring occasionally, until sauce is reduced and thickened.

Return guinea fowl, bacon, mushrooms and shallots to dish and season with salt and pepper. Bring to a boil, reduce heat and simmer 4 or 5 minutes to warm through. Cut guinea fowl in half with kitchen scissors or a sharp knife. Garnish with marjoram sprigs and serve.

Makes 4 servings.

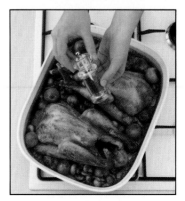

BOBOTIE

1 cup milk
1 thick slice white bread
1 tablespoon olive oil
1 large onion, chopped
2-1/4lbs. ground beef
2 teaspoons apricot jelly
1/4 cup lemon juice
1/2 cup raisins
10 dried apricots
2 tablespoons mild curry powder
12 blanched almonds, roughly chopped
1 teaspoon salt
Freshly ground pepper
6 bay leaves
2 eggs

Preheat oven to 350F (180C). Put half of the milk in a shallow dish, add bread and soak 5 minutes. Heat oil in a flameproof casserole dish. Add onion and cook, stirring occasionally, 5 minutes, or until soft. Squeeze milk from bread and add bread to dish with all remaining ingredients except eggs and remaining milk. Mix well then level surface with a spoon. Bake 30 minutes.

Beat together remaining milk and eggs and pour over meat. Return to oven and bake 20 to 25 minutes, or until custard has set.

Makes 6 to 8 servings.

Note: This dish is particularly good served with a fruit chutney.

—— POT ROAST OF BRISKET ——

1 (3-lb.) brisket of beef
2 leeks, thickly sliced
1 bay leaf
2 parsley stalks
1 celery leaf
1 lb. carrots, thickly sliced
1 lb. sweet potatoes, cut into chunks
1/4 cup cider vinegar
1/2 head cabbage, thickly shredded
Salt and freshly ground pepper

Heat a large flameproof casserole dish over medium heat, add beef and cook, turning, 3 or 4 minutes, or until browned all over.

Remove from dish. Add leeks to dish. With a piece of string, tie together bay leaf, parsley stalks and celery leaf and add to dish with carrots and sweet potatoes. Stir well. Add vinegar and 1/2 cup water. Put beef on top.

Cover and simmer 2-1/2 hours or until beef is tender. Remove beef from dish and keep warm. Remove vegetables with a slotted spoon and keep warm. Bring sauce to a boil and add cabbage. Season and simmer 5 minutes. Carve beef and serve with vegetables.

Makes 6 to 8 servings.

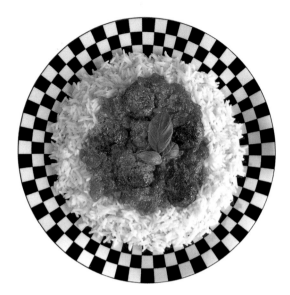

-MEATBALLS IN TOMATO SAUCE-

1/4 cup milk
1 egg, beaten
1/2 teaspoon freshly grated nutmeg
1 slice white bread
2 onions, finely chopped
2 garlic cloves, crushed
1 teaspoon dried thyme
2 tablespoons chopped fresh parsley
1 lb. lean ground beef
1 tablespoon olive oil
1 (14-oz.) can crushed tomatoes
2 tablespoons tomato paste
Salt and freshly ground pepper
Basil leaves, to garnish

In a shallow dish, mix together milk, egg and nutmeg. Add bread and soak 5 minutes. In a bowl, mix half of the onions and garlic with thyme, parsley and ground beef. Squeeze liquid from bread and add bread to beef mixture. Mix well and shape into 30 balls. Heat oil in a flameproof casserole dish. Add meatballs in batches and cook, turning, about 8 minutes, or until browned all over. Remove with a slotted spoon, drain on paper towels and keep warm.

Add remaining onion and garlic to dish with crushed tomatoes, tomato paste, salt and pepper. Bring to a boil and cook over medium heat, stirring constantly, until reduced and thickened. Add meatballs and heat gently to warm through. Garnish and serve.

Makes 4 servings.

— BEEF GOULASH WITH CHILE —

2 tablespoons olive oil
1 onion, sliced
1 garlic clove, crushed
2 teaspoons paprika
1-1/2 lbs. lean beef chuck, cubed
Pinch of caraway seeds
2 bay leaves
1 tablespoon balsamic vinegar
2 cups beef stock
Salt and freshly ground pepper
1-1/2 lbs. potatoes, diced
2 green bell peppers, sliced
1 fresh green chile, seeded and sliced
1 (14-oz.) can crushed tomatoes
2 tablespoons tomato paste

Heat oil in a flameproof casserole dish. Add onion, garlic and paprika and cook, stirring, 2 minutes. Add beef and cook 3 or 4 minutes, or until onion is soft and beef has browned. Add caraway seeds, bay leaves, vinegar and half of the stock. Season with salt and pepper and bring to a boil. Reduce heat, cover and simmer 1 hour.

Stir in remaining stock, potatoes, bell peppers, chile, tomatoes and tomato paste. Bring to a boil, reduce heat, cover and simmer 30 to 40 minutes, or until meat and vegetables are tender. Remove and discard bay leaves.

Makes 4 servings.

—— BELGIAN HOTCHPOTCH ——

8oz. beef brisket, cubed
8oz. lamb shoulder, cubed
3oz. pork shoulder, cubed
2-1/4 cups chicken stock
2 bay leaves
Salt and freshly ground pepper
4oz. rutabaga, diced
10 small onions
8oz. Brussels sprouts
1-1/2lbs. potatoes, diced
1 large carrot, diced
8oz. pork chipolata sausages
2/3 cup crème fraîche

Put meat into a large flameproof casserole dish; pour in stock.

Add 2-1/4 cups water, bay leaves and 1 teaspoon salt. Bring to a boil, skimming any froth from surface. Cover tightly and simmer 2 hours. Add vegetables and cook 30 minutes, or until meat is tender. Remove meat and vegetables from dish with a slotted spoon and keep warm. Put sausages into dish and cook 10 minutes. Remove with a slotted spoon and add to meat and vegetables.

Bring sauce to a boil and boil until reduced by one-third. Season with salt and pepper, stir in crème fraîche and heat gently to warm through. Pour sauce over meat and vegetables and serve.

Makes 4 to 6 servings.

—SAUSAGE & BEAN CASSEROLE—

1 tablespoon olive oil
1 onion, thinly sliced
10 cooked chorizo or other sausages, cut into
  chunks
1 (14-oz.) can pinto beans, drained
1 (14-oz.) can cannellini beans, drained
1 (14-oz.) can crushed tomatoes
1 cup vegetable stock
Salt and freshly ground pepper
3 potatoes, thinly sliced

Preheat oven to 400F (205C). Heat oil in a flameproof casserole dish. Add onion and cook, stirring occasionally, 5 minutes, or until soft. Add sausages and cook 4 or 5 minutes.

Add beans, tomatoes, stock, salt and pepper and bring to a boil. Remove from heat and arrange sliced potatoes on top. Bake 40 to 45 minutes, or until potatoes are tender and golden brown. Serve hot.

Makes 4 servings.

— CHILE BEEF WITH NACHOS —

1 tablespoon olive oil
1 onion, chopped
1 garlic clove, crushed
1 lb. lean ground beef
1 (15-oz.) can red kidney beans, drained
1 green bell pepper, chopped
2 tablespoons tomato paste
2 teaspoons mild chile powder
5 oz. tortilla chips
1 cup (4 oz.) shredded mozzarella cheese
1 or 2 teaspoons paprika

Heat oil in a flameproof casserole dish. Add onion and garlic and cook, stirring occasionally, 5 minutes, or until soft. Add beef and cook 6 to 8 minutes, or until brown. Stir in kidney beans, bell pepper, tomato paste, chile powder and 2/3 cup water. Cover and simmer 10 to 15 minutes. Preheat oven to 400F (205C).

Uncover and cook 5 minutes, or until sauce is reduced and thickened. Arrange tortilla chips over top, sprinkle with mozzarella cheese and paprika and bake 20 minutes or until cheese is melted and golden. Serve hot.

Makes 4 servings.

VENISON RAGOÛT

1 tablespoon all-purpose flour
Salt and freshly ground pepper
2 lbs. venison chuck, cubed
1 tablespoon olive oil
1 garlic clove, chopped
1-1/4 cups beef stock
1 tablespoon balsamic vinegar
8 juniper berries
8 black peppercorns
4 whole cloves
1 (14-oz.) can crushed tomatoes
8 oz. baby carrots, trimmed
4 oz. button mushrooms
1 tablespoon chopped fresh parsley

Preheat oven to 350F (180C). Season flour with salt and pepper and use to coat venison. Heat oil in a large flameproof casserole dish. Add venison, remaining seasoned flour and garlic and cook, stirring, 4 or 5 minutes.

Add stock, vinegar, juniper berries, peppercorns, cloves, tomatoes and carrots. Bring to a boil, cover and bake 1 hour or until venison is tender. Add mushrooms and cook 15 minutes. Sprinkle with chopped parsley and serve hot.

Makes 6 to 8 servings.

—CURRIED LAMB WITH RAITA—

3 tablespoons olive oil
2 onions, finely chopped
1/2-inch piece ginger root, peeled and grated
3 garlic cloves, crushed
1 teaspoon mild chile powder
1-1/2 teaspoons turmeric
1-1/2 teaspoons ground coriander
1/2 teaspoon each ground cumin and garam masala
1 lb. lean lamb, cubed
1/2 cup plain yogurt
Salt and freshly ground pepper
Mint sprigs, to garnish
RAITA:
1-1/4 cups plain yogurt
1 cup diced cucumber
1 tablespoon chopped fresh mint

Heat oil in a flameproof casserole dish. Add onions and cook, stirring occasionally, 5 minutes, or until soft. Add ginger root, garlic, chile powder, turmeric, coriander, cumin and garam masala and cook, stirring, 2 minutes. Add lamb and cook, stirring, 2 minutes, or until browned.

Add yogurt, 1/2 cup water, salt and pepper and stir well. Bring to a boil, reduce heat and simmer 45 minutes. Meanwhile, make raita. Mix together yogurt, cucumber and chopped mint. Season with salt and pepper. Refrigerate until required. Garnish lamb with mint sprigs and serve with raita.

Makes 4 servings.

HARVEST CASSEROLE

2 tablespoons olive oil
4 pork blade chops
1 large onion, sliced
2 leeks, chopped
1 garlic clove, crushed
8oz. parsnips, cut into chunks
8oz. carrots, cut into chunks
1 teaspoon dried sage
2 tablespoons all-purpose flour
1-1/4 cups beef stock
1-1/4 cups apple juice
Salt and freshly ground pepper
2 small apples
1-1/2 cups self-rising flour
1 teaspoon mixed dried herbs
1/4 cup vegetable shortening

Preheat oven to 325F (165C). Heat oil in a large flameproof casserole dish. Add chops and cook 2 or 3 minutes on each side until browned. Remove from pan and drain on paper towels. Add onion, leeks and garlic and cook, stirring occasionally, 5 minutes, or until soft. Add parsnips, carrots and sage and cook 2 minutes. Add all-purpose flour and cook, stirring, 1 minute. Gradually stir in stock and apple juice. Season with salt and pepper and bring to a boil.

Replace chops, cover and bake 1-1/4 hours, or until pork is tender. Meanwhile, core and coarsely chop apples and set aside. Mix together self-rising flour, herbs, salt and pepper; cut in shortening. Add 3/4 cup water and stir to a firm dough. Divide dough into 8 small dumplings. Stir apples into casserole. Place dumplings on top, return to oven and cook, uncovered, 20 minutes. Serve hot.

Makes 4 servings.

—STUFFED PORK SHOULDER—

1 (3-lb.) rolled pork roast
Salt and freshly ground pepper
1 lb. potatoes, cut into chunks
1 lb. rutabaga, cut into chunks
1 lb. parsnips, cut into chunks
1 tablespoon olive oil
1 tablespoon cornstarch
2-1/4 cups vegetable stock
1 tablespoon mango chutney
Sage leaves, to garnish
STUFFING:
1 (6-oz.) can corned beef, finely chopped
2 cups fresh white bread crumbs
1 onion, finely chopped
1 teaspoon dried sage
1 tablespoon mango chutney

Preheat oven to 350F (180C). Open out pork and flatten. To make stuffing, mix together corned beef, bread crumbs, onion and sage. Add chutney and stir together. Spread stuffing along center of inside of pork. Roll pork to enclose stuffing and tie securely with kitchen string. Season with salt and pepper. Put in a flameproof casserole dish, cover with a lid or piece of foil and bake 2 hours, basting meat every 45 minutes. Increase oven temperature to 400F (205C).

Place potatoes, rutabaga and parsnips around meat. Drizzle vegetables with oil and season with salt and pepper. Cook, uncovered, 45 to 55 minutes, turning vegetables occasionally, until meat and vegetables are tender. Remove meat and vegetables and keep warm. Mix cornstarch with a little cold water and stir into cooking juices. Stir in stock and bring to a boil, stirring. Add chutney and simmer 3 or 4 minutes. Slice pork, garnish and serve with vegetables and sauce.

Makes 6 to 8 servings.

CARAWAY POT ROAST

1 tablespoon olive oil
1 (2-3/4-lb.) pork shoulder roast
2 large onions, chopped
1 lb. parsnips, cut into chunks
3 tablespoons caraway seeds
1/2 teaspoon freshly grated nutmeg
Salt and freshly ground pepper
1 cup chicken stock
1 cup red wine
Thyme sprigs, to garnish

Preheat oven to 350F (180C). Heat oil in a large flameproof casserole dish. Add pork and cook until browned all over.

Remove pork from dish. Add onions and parsnips and cook, stirring occasionally, 7 minutes, or until golden. Lay pork on top of vegetables. Mix together caraway seeds and nutmeg and sprinkle on top of pork. Season with salt and pepper. Pour stock and wine around pork. Cover tightly and bake 2 hours, or until pork is cooked through and tender. Remove pork from dish and keep warm.

Remove vegetables from dish with a slotted spoon. Bring sauce to a boil and boil until reduced and thickened. Skim any fat from surface of sauce. Season with salt and pepper. Slice meat, garnish with thyme sprigs and serve with vegetables and sauce.

Makes 6 to 8 servings.

——PROVENÇAL PORK CHOPS——

2 teaspoons capers, chopped
1/4 cup pitted ripe olives, chopped
8 sun-dried tomatoes, chopped
1 (2-oz.) can anchovies, drained and chopped
Juice of 2 lemons
2 garlic cloves, crushed
1/3 cup olive oil
1/4 cup chopped fresh parsley
Salt and freshly ground pepper
4 pork loin chops, each weighing 6 oz.
Basil sprigs, to garnish

Mix together capers, olives, tomatoes, anchovies and lemon juice. Add garlic, all but 1 tablespoon of olive oil, parsley, salt and pepper.

Heat remaining oil in a flameproof casserole dish. Add chops and cook 10 minutes on each side, until cooked through.

Pour tomato mixture over chops and bring to a boil. Simmer 5 minutes. Garnish with basil sprigs and serve.

Makes 4 servings.

─────────PORK WITH APPLES─────────

2 tablespoons olive oil
4 boneless pork loin chops, each weighing 6 oz.
1 lb. onions, sliced
2 garlic cloves, crushed
12 plum tomatoes, peeled and chopped
2/3 cup beef stock
1/4 cup red wine vinegar
1-1/2 lbs. crisp apples
2 tablespoons lemon juice
Salt and freshly ground pepper

Preheat oven to 350F (180C). Heat olive oil in a flameproof casserole dish. Add chops and cook 3 minutes on each side, until browned.

Remove chops and keep warm. Add onions to dish and cook, stirring occasionally, 5 minutes, or until soft. Add garlic and tomatoes. Return chops to dish and pour in stock and red wine vinegar. Bring to a boil. Meanwhile, peel apples and use a melon baller to cut out ball-shaped pieces. Put apple balls into a bowl of water with lemon juice, to prevent apple discoloring. Chop remaining apple and add to dish. Cover and bake 1 hour.

Remove chops from dish and keep warm. Pour sauce into a blender or food processor and process 1 minute. Season with salt and pepper. Return to dish with chops and apple balls. Cook over low heat 15 minutes, or until apple balls are just tender. Serve hot.

Makes 4 servings.

──── BARBECUE SPARE RIBS ────

2-1/4lbs. pork spareribs
1 large onion, finely chopped
3 garlic cloves, crushed
2 bay leaves
1 teaspoon ground cumin
1 teaspoon mild chile powder
3 tablespoons cider vinegar
2 tablespoons tomato ketchup
1 tablespoon soy sauce
2 tablespoons honey
1 (14-oz.) can crushed tomatoes
Salt and freshly ground pepper

Preheat oven to 400F (205C). Put spareribs into a flameproof casserole dish and bake 30 minutes.

Remove ribs with a slotted spoon and set aside. In a bowl, mix together onion, garlic, bay leaves, cumin, chile powder, cider vinegar, tomato ketchup, soy sauce, honey and tomatoes. Season with salt and pepper.

Stir tomato mixture into dish. Bring to a boil, reduce heat and simmer 5 minutes. Add ribs, turn to coat with sauce and cover. Return pan to oven and cook 30 minutes.

Makes 4 servings.

Variation: Use 4 pork chops instead of spareribs, if you prefer.

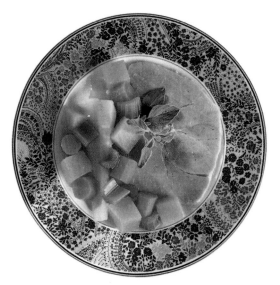

FRAGRANT HAM

1 (3-lb.) piece boneless, country-style ham
8oz. parsnips, halved lengthwise
1lb. carrots, cut into chunks
1lb. rutabaga, cut into chunks
2 stalks celery, cut into chunks
1 tablespoon brown sugar
1 tablespoon red wine vinegar
1 tablespoon black peppercorns
6 whole cloves
Oregano sprigs, to garnish

Put ham into a large flameproof casserole dish. Cover with cold water and soak 1 hour. Drain and cover with fresh water.

Add remaining ingredients to dish. Bring to a boil, reduce heat, cover and simmer 1-1/2 hours, or until ham is cooked through (170F, 75C in center).

Lift out ham, slice and arrange on warmed serving plates. Remove vegetables with a slotted spoon, arrange around ham, garnish with oregano sprigs and serve.

Makes 6 to 8 servings.

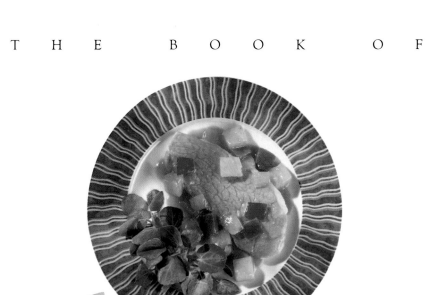

———— FRUITY HAM STEAKS ————

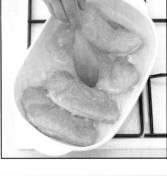

1/2-inch piece ginger root, peeled and grated
2 tablespoons tomato ketchup
1 tablespoon light brown sugar
1 tablespoon light soy sauce
1 tablespoon malt vinegar
1 tablespoon lemon juice
2 tablespoons olive oil
4 ham steaks, each weighing 6 oz.
1 green bell pepper, chopped
1 red bell pepper, chopped
1 onion, chopped
1 (8-oz.) can pineapple chunks in fruit juice,
   drained, with 2 tablespoons juice reserved
1 tablespoon cornstarch
Watercress, to garnish

In a bowl, mix together ginger root, tomato ketchup, brown sugar, soy sauce, vinegar and lemon juice. Set aside. Heat oil in a flameproof casserole dish. Add ham steaks and cook 5 minutes on each side.

Remove steaks from dish and keep warm. Add bell peppers and onion to dish and cook, stirring occasionally, 5 minutes, or until soft. Stir in ketchup mixture and pineapple chunks. Blend reserved pineapple juice with cornstarch. Add to dish and bring to a boil, stirring. Return steaks to dish and simmer 5 minutes. Garnish and serve.

Makes 4 servings.

— ZUCCHINI & HAM CASSEROLE —

1 lb. zucchini, finely grated
1 large onion, finely chopped
1/4 lb. ham, chopped
1-1/4 cups (5 oz.) shredded aged Cheddar cheese
1-1/4 cups self-rising flour
2/3 cup sunflower oil
5 eggs, beaten
Salt and freshly ground pepper

Preheat oven to 400F (205C). In a large bowl, mix together zucchini, onion, ham, cheese, flour, oil and eggs. Season with salt and pepper.

Lightly grease a shallow casserole dish. Add zucchini mixture and level surface. Bake 50 to 60 minutes, or until golden brown and firm. Cut into wedges and serve hot or cold.

Makes 4 to 6 servings.

— STUFFED CABBAGE LEAVES —

18 large cabbage leaves
2 onions, finely chopped
1/4 cup finely chopped fresh parsley
2 garlic cloves, crushed
8 oz. young spinach, shredded
8 oz. lean ground pork
1 lb. pork sausage
1/4 cup all-purpose flour
2 eggs, beaten
Salt and freshly ground pepper
12 slices bacon
2-1/4 cups chicken stock

Blanch cabbage leaves in boiling water 2 minutes. Remove and drain.

Preheat oven to 350F (180C). In a large bowl, mix together onions, parsley, garlic, spinach, ground pork and sausage. Add flour and eggs and mix well. Season with salt and pepper. Divide into 6 equal portions. Trim tough center core from each cabbage leaf. Arrange leaves in 6 piles of 3 leaves each.

Place a portion of filling on each pile of cabbage leaves. Fold each one into a package and wrap each one with 2 slices of bacon. Put into an casserole dish and add stock. Bring to a boil, cover and bake 1-1/2 hours. Remove with a slotted spoon, add a little cooking liquid and serve.

Makes 6 servings.

TOAD IN THE HOLE

1 cup all-purpose flour
Pinch of salt
1 teaspoon mixed dried herbs
1 egg, beaten
1-1/4 cups milk
1 tablespoon sunflower oil
1 small onion, chopped
1 lb. sausage links

Preheat oven to 400F (205C). In a large bowl, mix together flour, salt and herbs. Make a well in center and add egg and half of the milk. Beat to a smooth batter. Stir in remaining milk and mix until smooth.

Heat oil in a shallow flameproof casserole dish. Add onion and cook, stirring occasionally, 3 minutes. Add sausages and cook until browned and cooked through. Drain off excess fat.

Pour batter into dish and bake 30 minutes, or until batter is risen and golden. Serve immediately.

Makes 4 servings.

Variation: There are many types of sausages available. Try using different types to vary this recipe.

LAMB EN PAPILLOTTE

4 lamb leg steaks, each weighing 6 oz.
1 tablespoon Dijon mustard
4 green onions, sliced
1 teaspoon chopped fresh rosemary
Salt and freshly ground pepper
1 lb. sweet potatoes, cut into chunks
1 lb. zucchini, thickly sliced
1 tablespoon olive oil
Rosemary sprigs, to garnish

Preheat oven to 400F (205C). Cut four large squares of foil and place a lamb steak on each one. Spread lamb with mustard and sprinkle with green onions and rosemary. Season with salt and pepper.

Bring foil up over steaks to make a package and twist edges together to seal. Put packages in an ovenproof dish. Arrange sweet potatoes and zucchini around packages.

Drizzle vegetables with oil and season with salt and pepper. Bake 1 hour, basting and turning vegetables at least twice. Remove lamb from foil, garnish with rosemary and serve with vegetables.

Makes 4 servings.

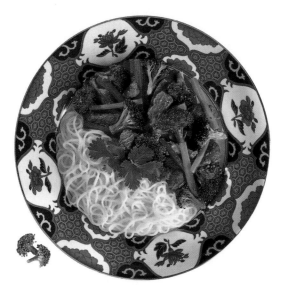

——ORANGE & GINGER LAMB——

2 tablespoons dark soy sauce
2 tablespoons dry sherry
1 tablespoon orange juice
2 garlic cloves, finely chopped
1/2-inch piece ginger root, peeled and grated
1 lb. lean lamb, cut into strips
2 tablespoons vegetable oil
4 oz. broccoli flowerets
8 oz. carrots, cut into matchsticks
1 red bell pepper, thinly sliced
1 teaspoon light brown sugar
Cilantro sprigs, to garnish

In a bowl, mix together soy sauce, sherry, orange juice, garlic and ginger root. Add lamb.

Turn to coat with marinade and refrigerate 2 or 3 hours. Drain lamb, reserving marinade. Heat oil in a flameproof casserole dish. Add lamb and cook, stirring, 8 to 10 minutes, or until browned and cooked through. Add broccoli, carrots and bell pepper and cook, stirring, 5 minutes.

Pour in reserved marinade and sugar and bring to a boil. Reduce heat, cover and simmer 5 minutes. Garnish with cilantro sprigs and serve immediately.

Makes 4 servings.

—— LAMB CHOPS & CABBAGE ——

1 tablespoon olive oil
4 lamb sirloin chops, each weighing 6 oz.
2 large onions, sliced
8 oz. Savoy cabbage, shredded
1 lb. potatoes, thinly sliced
Salt and freshly ground pepper
Fresh bouquet garni
2-1/4 cups chicken stock
2 tablespoons butter, melted
Chopped fresh parsley, to garnish

Heat oil in a flameproof casserole dish. Add chops and cook 2 or 3 minutes on each side until browned. Remove and set aside.

Preheat oven to 400F (205C). Add onions and cabbage to dish and cook over low heat 10 minutes, or until soft. Remove half of mixture and set aside. Place chops on top of remaining onion and cabbage mixture. Mix two-thirds of potatoes with reserved onion and cabbage mixture. Season with salt and pepper. Arrange on top of chops, placing bouquet garni in middle. Add stock to dish.

Arrange remaining potatoes on top and brush with melted butter. Bake 15 minutes. Remove from oven and press potatoes down. Brush again with melted butter and season with salt and pepper. Reduce oven temperature to 350F (180C) and cook 1 hour or until lamb and potatoes are tender. Garnish with chopped parsley and serve.

Makes 4 servings.

——MEDITERRANEAN LAMB——

1 eggplant, sliced
2 teaspoons salt
2 tablespoons olive oil, plus extra for brushing
1 lb. lean lamb, cubed
2 leeks, sliced
1 green bell pepper, chopped
1 (14-oz.) can crushed tomatoes
1 garlic clove, crushed
2 zucchini, sliced
1 tablespoon tomato paste
1 tablespoon chopped fresh rosemary

Place eggplant in a colander, sprinkle with salt and let stand 30 minutes.

Preheat oven to 375F (190C). Heat oil in a flameproof casserole dish. Add lamb and cook, stirring, 3 or 4 minutes, or until browned. Add leeks and cook, stirring, 4 or 5 minutes, or until soft. Stir in bell pepper, tomatoes, garlic, zucchini, tomato paste and rosemary. Simmer 5 to 10 minutes.

Rinse eggplant in cold water and pat dry with paper towels. Arrange eggplant slices on top of lamb mixture and brush with olive oil. Bake 30 to 40 minutes, or until eggplant slices are golden brown and tender. Serve hot.

Makes 4 servings.

– RACK OF LAMB WITH ONIONS –

Grated zest of 1 lemon
1 tablespoon chopped fresh parsley
2 teaspoons minced garlic
1 tablespoon chopped fresh rosemary
Salt and freshly ground pepper
1 (8-bone) rack of lamb
8 small onions, peeled
1 tablespoon olive oil
1 cup vegetable stock
3 tablespoons red wine vinegar
2 tablespoons sugar
Rosemary sprigs, to garnish

Preheat oven to 400F (205C). In a small bowl, mix together lemon zest, parsley, garlic, rosemary, salt and pepper.

Put lamb, fat side up, in a flameproof casserole dish. Spread lemon and herb mixture over lamb. Place onions in dish and brush with oil. Roast 20 minutes. Turn off heat and leave lamb and onions in oven 20 minutes. Remove from dish and keep warm.

Add stock, vinegar and sugar to dish. Season with plenty of black pepper. Bring to a boil and boil, stirring, until liquid has reduced by half and thickened. Return onions to dish, turn in sauce and simmer 5 minutes. Cut lamb into individual chops, garnish and serve with onions and sauce.

Makes 4 servings.

Note: If you prefer more well-done, roast lamb an extra 5 to 10 minutes, according to taste.

SAGE LAMB COBBLER

2 lbs. neck of lamb, boned and cubed
1/4 cup all-purpose flour
1 tablespoon olive oil
1 large onion, chopped
1/4 cup dried peas, soaked overnight
8 oz. each carrots and rutabaga, diced
2-1/4 cups chicken stock
Salt and freshly ground pepper
Large pinch of paprika
TOPPING:
2 cups all-purpose flour
1-1/2 teaspoons baking powder
1/4 cup butter
1 teaspoon dried sage
1 egg
2 tablespoons milk, plus extra for brushing

Preheat oven to 325F (160C). Coat lamb in flour. Heat oil in a flameproof casserole dish. Add lamb and cook , stirring, until browned. Remove and set aside. Add onion and cook, stirring occasionally, 7 minutes, or until lightly browned. Return lamb and add peas, carrots and rutabaga. Pour in stock and season with salt, pepper and paprika. Bring to a boil, cover and bake 2 hours. Sift flour, baking powder and salt into a bowl. Cut in butter until mixture resembles fine bread crumbs.

Stir in sage. Add egg and milk and stir to a soft dough. Knead on a lightly floured surface and roll out to 1/2-inch thickness. Using a pastry cutter, cut out 1-1/2-inch rounds. Arrange rounds on top of dish and brush with milk. Increase oven temperature to 400F (205C). Return dish to oven and cook, uncovered, 15 to 20 minutes, or until biscuits are risen and golden. Serve.

Makes 6 to 8 servings.

VEAL WITH MUSHROOMS

2 tablespoons olive oil
4 slices bacon, cut into thin strips
4 slices veal shank, each weighing 8 oz.
12 oz. carrots, cut into thick strips
4 plum tomatoes, peeled, quartered and seeded
2-1/2 cups beef stock
1/2 cup red wine
1 lb. mixed mushrooms
1/4 cup butter, diced
1/4 cup chopped fresh parsley

Heat oil in a flameproof casserole dish. Add bacon and cook 3 or 4 minutes. Remove and drain on paper towels. Add veal and cook until browned on both sides.

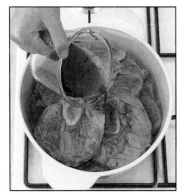

Remove veal and drain on paper towels. Add carrots and tomatoes to dish and cook 2 or 3 minutes. Return veal to dish. Add stock and red wine. Bring to a boil, reduce heat, cover and simmer 40 minutes. Add mushrooms and bacon and cook 10 minutes, or until veal is tender.

Lift out veal and remove carrots, mushrooms and bacon with a slotted spoon. Keep warm. Strain sauce and return to pan. Bring to a boil and boil until reduced by one-third. Whisk in butter, a little at a time. Stir in parsley. Return bacon and vegetables to sauce and cook over low heat 2 minutes to warm through. Arrange veal on warmed serving plates, pour sauce over veal and serve.

Makes 4 servings.

BAKED EGGS IN NESTS

1-1/2 lbs. waxy potatoes, halved
8 oz. broccoli flowerets
2 zucchini
2 leeks, thinly sliced
1 tablespoon Worcestershire sauce
Salt and freshly ground pepper
4 eggs

Cook potatoes in boiling salted water 5 to 10 minutes. Add broccoli and cook 5 minutes. Drain.

Coarsely grate potatoes. Using a vegetable peeler, cut zucchini lengthwise into ribbons. Mix together potatoes, broccoli, leeks, zucchini and Worcestershire sauce. Season with salt and pepper. Lightly oil a flameproof casserole dish and add vegetable mixture.

Make four wells in vegetable mixture and break an egg into each one. Cover and cook very gently 10 minutes, or until eggs have set. Serve immediately.

Makes 2 to 4 servings.

—FENNEL & BEAN CASSEROLE—

1-1/4 cups dried haricot beans, soaked overnight
1 tablespoon olive oil
2 onions, chopped
2 garlic cloves, crushed
1 head of celery, sliced
2 fennel bulbs, thinly sliced
2 tablespoons tomato paste
2 tablespoons chopped fresh oregano
1 tablespoon chopped fresh thyme
2 bay leaves
2 teaspoons each salt and sugar
2 (14-oz.) cans crushed tomatoes
Freshly ground pepper
6 slices day-old bread, made into crumbs
Thyme sprigs, to garnish

Put haricot beans into a flameproof casserole dish. Cover with cold water. Bring to a boil and boil rapidly 10 minutes. Cover and simmer 1 hour. Drain and set aside. Heat oil in dish. Add onions and garlic and cook, stirring occasionally, 5 minutes, or until soft. Add beans, celery, fennel, tomato paste, half of the oregano, the thyme, bay leaves, salt, sugar and tomatoes. Season with pepper. Cover and simmer 30 minutes or until vegetables are tender.

Preheat oven to 425F (220C). Mix together bread crumbs and remaining oregano and scatter over top of bean mixture. Bake 15 to 20 minutes, or until bread crumbs are golden brown. Garnish with thyme sprigs and serve.

Makes 4 to 6 servings.

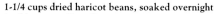

LEEK & CHEESE PIE

1lb. leeks, chopped
1 teaspoon salt
1/4 cup butter
2 large onions, sliced
2 bunches green onions, sliced
1 cup (4oz.) crumbled feta cheese
2 eggs, beaten
Freshly ground pepper
8 sheets filo pastry
1/4 cup melted butter

Put leeks into a colander, sprinkle with salt and leave 30 minutes. Squeeze dry.

Heat butter in a flameproof casserole dish. Add onions and green onions and cook, stirring occasionally, 3 to 5 minutes, or until soft but not colored. Remove from heat and let cool 10 minutes. Preheat oven to 400F (205C). Add leeks, feta cheese and eggs to onion mixture, season with pepper and mix well.

Crumple sheets of filo pastry and arrange on top of leek mixture. Brush with melted butter and bake 30 to 35 minutes, or until pastry is golden brown. Serve.

Makes 4 to 6 servings.

Note: To prepare leeks, cut off dark green tops and root ends. Slice white part almost in half lengthwise, then rinse under cold running water to remove sand.

VEGETABLE BIRYANI

2 tablespoons sunflower oil
1 lb. onions, sliced
3 carrots, diced
1 medium potato, diced
1-inch piece ginger root, peeled and grated
2 garlic cloves, crushed
1 tablespoon hot curry paste
1 teaspoon turmeric
1/2 teaspoon ground cinnamon
1 cup long grain rice
4-1/4 cups hot vegetable stock
4 oz. cauliflower flowerets
Salt and freshly ground pepper
4 oz. frozen green peas
1/2 cup toasted cashew nuts
2 tablespoons chopped fresh cilantro

Heat half oil in a large flameproof casserole dish. Add half of the onions and cook, stirring occasionally, 10 to 15 minutes, or until crisp and golden. Remove with a slotted spoon, drain on paper towels and set aside. Heat remaining oil in dish and add carrots, potato and remaining onions. Stir in ginger root, garlic, curry paste, turmeric and cinnamon and cook, stirring, 5 minutes.

Add rice and stir 1 minute. Pour in stock and bring to a boil. Stir in cauliflower, salt and pepper. Cover and simmer 15 minutes. Stir in peas, cashews and cilantro. Cover and cook 5 minutes or until rice is tender and liquid has been absorbed. Scatter reserved onions over top and serve.

Makes 4 servings.

ZUCCHINI GOUGÈRE

2 tablespoons olive oil
5 zucchini, thinly sliced
10 oz. button mushrooms
2 leeks, thinly sliced
2 teaspoons whole-grain mustard
1-1/4 cups crème fraîche
Salt and freshly ground pepper
CHOUX PASTRY:
1/4 cup butter
2 cups all-purpose flour
2 eggs, beaten

To make choux pastry, melt butter in 2/3 cup water, then bring quickly to a boil. Remove from heat and immediately stir in flour.

Beat well until mixture is smooth and comes away from sides of pan. Return to heat and cook over low heat, stirring, 2 or 3 minutes. Remove from heat and gradually add eggs, beating well. Set aside. Preheat oven to 425F (220C). Heat oil in a flameproof casserole dish. Add zucchini, button mushrooms and leeks and cook, stirring occasionally, 6 to 8 minutes, or until tender.

Stir in mustard and crème fraîche and season with salt and pepper. Put choux pastry in a pastry bag fitted with a plain 1/2-inch tip. Pipe small balls of pastry around edge of zucchini mixture. Bake 20 to 30 minutes, or until pastry is risen and golden. Serve hot.

Makes 4 to 6 servings.

— VEGETABLE & CHEESE BAKE —

6 thick slices whole-wheat bread
2 zucchini, sliced
1 beefsteak tomato, chopped
6 oz. mushrooms, chopped
1-3/4 cups milk
5 eggs, beaten
1 tablespoon chopped fresh chives
Salt and freshly ground pepper
1-1/4 cups (5 oz.) shredded Cheddar cheese
Flat-leaf parsley sprigs, to garnish

Preheat oven to 400F (205C). Cut bread into strips. Arrange half of bread in a shallow ovenproof dish.

Spread zucchini, tomato and mushrooms over bread and top with remaining bread. In a large bowl, mix together milk and eggs. Add chives and season with salt and pepper.

Pour milk mixture over bread. Sprinkle cheese over top and bake 50 minutes, or until egg mixture has set and topping is golden brown. Garnish with flat-leaf parsley and serve immediately.

Makes 4 servings.

——MOROCCAN CASSEROLE——

2 tablespoons olive oil
1 large onion, chopped
1 large eggplant, cut into chunks
2 garlic cloves, crushed
1 teaspoon ground cumin
1 teaspoon turmeric
1 teaspoon ground ginger
1 teaspoon paprika
1 teaspoon ground allspice
3 (14-oz.) cans crushed tomatoes
1 (1-lb.) can chickpeas, drained
1/2 cup raisins
1 tablespoon chopped fresh cilantro
3 tablespoons chopped fresh parsley
Salt and freshly ground pepper

Heat oil in a flameproof casserole dish. Add onion and cook, stirring occasionally, 5 minutes, or until soft. Add eggplant, cover and cook 5 minutes. Add garlic, cumin, turmeric, ginger, paprika and allspice and cook, stirring, 1 minute.

Stir in tomatoes, chickpeas, raisins, cilantro and parsley. Season with salt and pepper. Bring to a boil, reduce heat and simmer 45 minutes or until vegetables are tender. Serve hot.

Makes 4 to 6 servings.

── MUSHROOM & NUT PILAF ──

3 tablespoons butter
2 oz. pine nuts
2 oz. sunflower kernels
1 onion, chopped
2 leeks, chopped
1 red bell pepper, chopped
1 carrot, diced
1 cup Arborio rice
4-1/2 cups vegetable stock
4 oz. button mushrooms, sliced
Salt and freshly ground pepper

Heat 1 tablespoon of the butter in a flameproof casserole dish. Add pine nuts and sunflower kernels and cook until golden.

Remove seeds from dish with a slotted spoon and set aside. Heat remaining butter in dish. Add onion, leeks, bell pepper and carrot and cook, stirring occasionally, 3 minutes. Add rice and cook, stirring, 2 minutes. Add stock, cover and bring to a boil. Simmer 30 minutes or until most of liquid is absorbed and rice is just tender.

Add mushrooms, pine nuts and sunflower kernels and cook over low heat, stirring frequently, 10 minutes. Season with salt and pepper and serve.

Makes 4 servings.

– LEEK STEW WITH DUMPLINGS –

1-1/2 lbs. leeks, halved lengthwise
12 oz. potatoes, diced
8 oz. Jerusalem artichokes, peeled and quartered
4-1/2 cups vegetable stock
Salt
Fresh chives, to garnish
DUMPLINGS:
1 cup self-rising flour
2 tablespoons chopped fresh chives
2 tablespoons vegetable shortening

Cut leeks into 3-inch lengths. Put leeks, potatoes and artichokes in a large flameproof casserole dish.

Add stock and season with salt. Bring to a boil, reduce heat, cover and simmer 45 to 60 minutes or until tender. Meanwhile, to make dumplings, put flour, chives and salt in a large bowl; cut in shortening until mixture resembles coarse crumbs. Stir in 1/4 cup water and stir to a dough. Knead lightly and rest 5 minutes.

Shape dough into 8 small dumplings. Place dumplings around outside of vegetable mixture. Cover and simmer 30 minutes. Garnish with chives and serve.

Makes 4 servings.

— STIR-FRIED SPINACH & TOFU —

1 tablespoon olive oil
2 stalks celery, sliced
10 green onions, sliced
1-inch piece ginger root, peeled and thinly sliced
8 oz. smoked tofu
6 oz. snow peas
1 lb. spinach, torn
1 tablespoon black bean sauce
Freshly ground pepper
2 tablespoons toasted sesame seeds

Heat oil in a flameproof casserole dish. Add celery, green onions and ginger root and stir-fry 3 or 4 minutes, or until soft.

Add tofu and snow peas and stir-fry 2 or 3 minutes. Gradually add spinach and stir-fry 8 to 10 minutes, or until wilted and tender.

Stir in black bean sauce and mix well. Season with pepper. Stir in sesame seeds and serve.

Makes 4 servings.

VEGETABLE COBBLER

1 tablespoon olive oil
1 garlic clove, crushed
2 leeks, thinly sliced
2 teaspoons mustard seeds
8oz. mushrooms, sliced
8oz. broccoli flowerets
6oz. fresh or frozen green peas
1-1/4 cups half-and-half
Large pinch of freshly grated nutmeg
1 teaspoon prepared English mustard
1 tablespoon chopped fresh parsley
7oz. puff pastry, thawed if frozen
Milk for brushing

Heat oil in a flameproof casserole dish. Add garlic and leeks and cook until soft.

Add mustard seeds and cook until they start to pop. Add mushrooms, broccoli and peas. Cover and cook 8 to 10 minutes, or until tender. Remove from heat. Stir in half-and-half, nutmeg, mustard and parsley. Preheat oven to 425F (220C).

Roll out pastry on a lightly floured surface. Using a pastry cutter, cut out 12 (2-inch) rounds. Arrange on top of vegetable mixture. Brush with a little milk and bake 30 to 35 minutes, or until risen and golden. Serve hot.

Makes 4 to 6 servings.

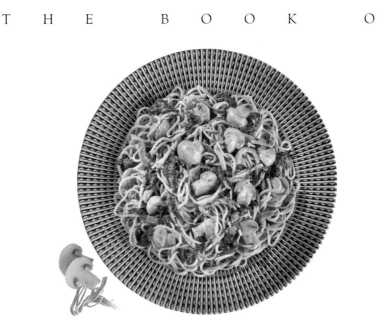

—— NOODLES WITH SPINACH ——

2 tablespoons olive oil
1 red onion, thinly sliced
10 oz. button mushrooms, halved
12 oz. spinach, torn
8 oz. thread egg noodles
1 (8-oz.) package cream cheese with garlic and
  herbs
Salt and freshly ground pepper

Heat oil in a flameproof casserole dish. Add onion and cook, stirring occasionally, 5 minutes, or until soft. Add mushrooms and spinach and cook, stirring occasionally, 10 to 15 minutes, or until spinach is wilted and mushrooms tender.

Meanwhile, put noodles into a large bowl and cover with boiling water. Leave 4 or 5 minutes, or until tender. Drain. Add cheese to spinach mixture and heat gently, stirring, until melted.

Add noodles to vegetable and cheese, season with salt and pepper and mix well. Serve hot.

Makes 4 servings.

SPANISH OMELET

2 tablespoons olive oil
1 onion, thinly sliced
12 oz. potatoes, diced
1 red bell pepper, thinly sliced
1 green bell pepper, thinly sliced
6 eggs, beaten
1 tablespoon chopped fresh parsley
Salt and freshly ground pepper

Heat oil in a shallow flameproof casserole dish. Add onion and potatoes and cook, stirring occasionally, 6 to 8 minutes, or until potatoes are tender. Stir in bell peppers and cook 2 or 3 minutes.

Beat together eggs, parsley, salt and pepper and pour into dish. Cook over low heat 3 or 4 minutes, or until eggs have set on bottom. Preheat broiler.

Put omelet under broiler and cook 5 or 6 minutes, or until eggs have set. Cut into wedges and serve hot or at room temperature.

Makes 4 servings.

MIXED VEGETABLE RÖSTI

1 tablespoon olive oil
1 onion, sliced
8 oz. green beans, trimmed
8 oz. cauliflowerets
4 tomatoes, peeled and quartered
1 tablespoon chopped fresh parsley
Salt and freshly ground pepper
1-1/2 lbs. potatoes, grated
1 cup (4 oz.) shredded mozzarella cheese

Heat oil in a flameproof casserole dish. Add onion and cook, stirring occasionally, 5 minutes, or until soft. Preheat oven to 400F (205C).

Add beans, cauliflower and tomatoes and cook, stirring occasionally, 10 minutes, or until tender. Stir in parsley and season with salt and pepper.

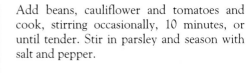

Spread potatoes over vegetables and top with cheese. Bake 30 minutes, or until potatoes are tender and cheese is melted and golden. Serve hot.

Makes 4 servings.

Note: Waxy potatoes should be used for this recipe.

—SPICED FRUITY COUSCOUS—

2 tablespoons olive oil
2 tablespoons butter
6 green onions, finely chopped
2 cups vegetable stock
2 tablespoons mild curry powder
1 teaspoon sugar
1 generous cup couscous
2 tablespoons chopped fresh chives
1 small green apple, cored and finely diced
2 oz. pine nuts

Heat oil and butter in a flameproof casserole dish. Add green onions and cook over low heat until soft. Add stock, curry powder and sugar.

Bring to a boil. Add couscous and stir well. Put lid on dish, turn off heat and let stand 30 minutes, or until stock has been absorbed and couscous is tender.

Add chives, apple and pine nuts and stir well. Serve immediately.

Makes 2 to 4 servings.

—NUT BAKE WITH TOMATOES—

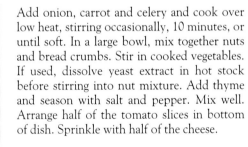

2 tablespoons butter
1 onion, finely chopped
1 large carrot, finely chopped
2 stalks celery, finely chopped
2-1/2 cups finely chopped mixed nuts
2 cups fresh whole-wheat bread crumbs
2 teaspoons yeast extract (optional)
1-1/4 cups hot vegetable stock
2 teaspoons dried thyme
Salt and freshly ground pepper
2 beefsteak tomatoes, sliced
1 cup (4oz.) shredded aged Cheddar cheese

Preheat oven to 350F (180C). Heat butter in a flameproof casserole dish.

Add onion, carrot and celery and cook over low heat, stirring occasionally, 10 minutes, or until soft. In a large bowl, mix together nuts and bread crumbs. Stir in cooked vegetables. If used, dissolve yeast extract in hot stock before stirring into nut mixture. Add thyme and season with salt and pepper. Mix well. Arrange half of the tomato slices in bottom of dish. Sprinkle with half of the cheese.

Spread half of the nut mixture on top. Add remaining tomato slices and cover with remaining nut mixture. Sprinkle with remaining cheese and bake 50 to 60 minutes, or until cheese is melted and golden. Serve hot.

Makes 4 servings.

-SUN-DRIED TOMATO RISOTTO-

1/4 cup butter
1 tablespoon olive oil
2 red onions, chopped
12 sun-dried tomatoes, chopped
1 tablespoon pesto sauce
1 cup Arborio rice
4-1/2 cups vegetable stock
8 oz. mushrooms, sliced
Salt and freshly ground pepper
2 oz. Parmesan cheese
Chopped fresh flat-leaf parsley, to garnish

Heat butter and oil in a flameproof casserole dish. Add onions and cook, stirring occasionally, 5 minutes, or until soft.

Add sun-dried tomatoes and pesto sauce and cook 3 or 4 minutes. Add rice and cook, stirring, 1 minute. Stir in about one-third of stock and simmer, stirring occasionally, until most of liquid has been absorbed.

Stir in mushrooms and season with salt and pepper. Add half of the remaining stock and simmer, stirring occasionally. When most of liquid has been absorbed, stir in remaining stock and simmer until all liquid has been absorbed and rice is tender and creamy. Using a vegetable peeler, shave curls of Parmesan cheese over risotto, sprinkle with parsley and serve.

Makes 2 to 4 servings.

LENTIL & BEAN CHILE

1 tablespoon olive oil
1 onion, chopped
1 garlic clove, chopped
3/4 cup green lentils
1-1/4 cups vegetable stock
1 teaspoon mild chile powder
1 (14-oz.) can crushed tomatoes
1 (15-oz.) can red kidney beans, drained
1 green bell pepper, chopped
Salt and freshly ground pepper
Chopped fresh flat-leaf parsley, to garnish

Heat oil in a flameproof casserole dish. Add onion and garlic and cook until soft. Add lentils, stock, chile powder and tomatoes.

Cover and simmer 30 to 40 minutes, or until lentils are almost cooked.

Stir in kidney beans and bell pepper and simmer 10 to 15 minutes, or until lentils are tender and liquid has been absorbed. Season with salt and pepper. Garnish with chopped parsley and serve.

Makes 4 servings.

VEGETABLE CHILE

2 onions
5 large fresh red chiles, seeded and chopped
1 red bell pepper, chopped
1 large garlic clove, chopped
2 tablespoons dry white wine
Salt
1 tablespoon olive oil
1 green bell pepper, thinly sliced
1 tablespoon tomato paste
1 teaspoon ground cumin
1 (8-oz.) can red kidney beans, drained
Basil sprigs, to garnish

Roughly chop one of the onions. Put into a food processor with chiles, red bell pepper, garlic, wine and salt.

Process 2 minutes or until pureed. Slice remaining onion. Heat oil in a flameproof casserole dish, add sliced onion and cook, stirring occasionally, 5 minutes, or until soft. Add pureed mixture, 2 tablespoons water and green bell pepper.

Bring to a boil, reduce heat, cover and simmer 30 minutes. Add tomato paste, cumin and kidney beans. Simmer 10 to 15 minutes. Garnish with basil and serve.

Makes 2 to 4 servings.

VEGETABLE FRICASSÉE

1-3/4 cups vegetable stock
12 oz. rutabaga, cut into chunks
8 oz. each carrots and potatoes, cut into chunks
1 leek, sliced
8 oz. cauliflowerets
8 oz. green beans
1/4 cup butter
1/2 cup whole-wheat flour
2/3 cup milk
3/4 cup chopped fresh parsley
1 teaspoon lemon juice
Salt and freshly ground pepper

Pour stock into a flameproof casserole dish and bring to a boil. Add rutabaga, carrots and potatoes.

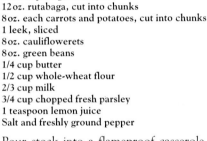

Return to a boil and cook 5 minutes. Add leek, cauliflower and beans and cook 3 to 5 minutes. Drain vegetables, reserving stock. Heat butter in dish. Stir in flour and cook, stirring, 1 minute. Gradually stir in milk and 1 cup of reserved stock, stirring constantly until smooth.

Reduce heat, stir in parsley and lemon juice and season with salt and pepper. Add vegetables and cook 4 or 5 minutes, to warm through. Serve hot.

Makes 4 servings.

MUSHROOM GRATIN

1 tablespoon butter
1 garlic clove, crushed
2 lbs. potatoes, thinly sliced
6 oz. brown mushrooms, sliced
4 oz. button mushrooms, sliced
Salt and freshly ground pepper
2 eggs, beaten
2/3 cup milk
2/3 cup crème fraîche
1-1/2 cups (6 oz.) shredded gruyère cheese
Chopped fresh parsley, to garnish

Preheat oven to 400F (205C). Rub an ovenproof dish with butter and garlic. Add half of the potatoes and mushrooms.

Top with remaining potatoes. Season generously with salt and pepper. Mix together eggs, milk and crème fraîche and pour over vegetables. Bake 1 hour.

Sprinkle cheese over top and bake 25 minutes, or until cheese is melted and golden and vegetables are tender. Garnish with parsley and serve.

Makes 4 servings.

— BAKED PANETTONE PUDDING —

3 eggs, beaten
1/2 cup sugar
1-3/4 cups whole milk
1 teaspoon vanilla extract
6 slices panettone with dried fruit or other rich yeast
   bread
1/4 cup orange marmalade
Powdered sugar for dusting

In a large bowl, beat eggs and sugar until light and foamy. Add milk and vanilla extract and mix well.

Lightly butter a shallow ovenproof dish. Spread slices of panettone with orange marmalade. Sandwich together, 2 pieces at a time, and cut pieces in half. Arrange in dish. Ladle egg mixture over panettone and soak 15 minutes.

Preheat oven to 325F (165C). Place dish in a larger ovenproof dish or roasting pan and pour in enough boiling water to come halfway up sides of dish. Bake 50 minutes, or until custard is set and top is golden with a slight crust. Sprinkle with powdered sugar and serve hot or cold.

Makes 4 to 6 servings.

FLAMBÉED FRUIT

1/4 cup butter
1/4 cup sugar
2 oranges, peeled and segmented
1 (12-oz.) can pineapple chunks in fruit juice
4 bananas, thickly sliced
1 tablespoon orange liqueur or brandy
Mint sprigs, to garnish

Put butter and sugar in a flameproof casserole dish and cook over low heat until melted and a caramel color.

Add oranges, pineapple chunks and their juice and bananas. Bring to a boil and boil 5 minutes or until sauce thickens.

Put liqueur or brandy in a ladle and warm gently. Set alight and pour over fruit. Cook 1 minute, until flames die down. Garnish with mint and serve warm.

Makes 4 servings.

RHUBARB MERINGUE

1 lb. rhubarb, sliced
4 bananas, sliced
1/4 cup packed light brown sugar
1/2 teaspoon ground cinnamon
Grated zest and juice of 3 oranges
MERINGUE:
3 egg whites
3/4 cup sugar

Preheat oven to 350F (180C). Put rhubarb and bananas in an ovenproof dish. Sprinkle with brown sugar, cinnamon and orange zest. Add orange juice, making sure fruit is evenly coated.

Cover with a lid or piece of foil and bake 15 to 20 minutes or until fruit is tender. Meanwhile, to make meringue, beat egg whites until they form stiff peaks. Beat in sugar.

Put meringue into a pastry bag with a star tip and pipe over fruit. Return to oven and cook 20 minutes or until meringue is crisp and golden. Serve warm or cold.

Makes 4 to 6 servings.

──── BAKED APPLES IN BATTER ────

2 tablespoons corn syrup
4 sweet apples, cored
8 bay leaves
Powdered sugar for dusting
BATTER:
1/2 cup all-purpose flour
2 eggs, beaten
1 teaspoon vanilla extract
1-1/4 cups milk
1/4 cup sugar
1 tablespoon butter, melted

Preheat oven to 375F (190C). Lightly butter an ovenproof dish and spread corn syrup over bottom.

Place apples on top of corn syrup. Put a bay leaf in cavity of each apple, reserving 4 remaining leaves for decoration. Bake 15 minutes. Meanwhile, make batter. Sift flour into a large bowl and make a well in center. Add eggs, vanilla extract and a little milk. Beat into flour, gradually adding more milk to form a smooth batter. Stir in sugar and melted butter.

Pour batter over apples and bake 45 to 50 minutes, or until batter is risen and golden. Remove bay leaves from apples. Decorate with reserved bay leaves, dust with powdered sugar and serve.

Makes 4 servings.

- RICE PUDDING WITH PEACHES -

3-3/4 cups whole milk
6 cardamom pods
1/2 cup short grain rice
1/2 cup pistachio nuts, chopped
1/2 cup packed light brown sugar
1/4 cup butter, diced
2 egg yolks
1 (14-oz.) can peach halves, drained

Pour milk into a flameproof casserole dish. Add cardamom pods, bring to a boil, reduce heat and simmer 5 minutes. Remove cardamom pods. Stir in rice.

Return to a boil, reduce heat and simmer, stirring frequently, 15 to 20 minutes, or until rice is tender and most of liquid has been absorbed. Remove from heat and stir in pistachio nuts, half of the brown sugar, the butter and egg yolks. Let cool slightly. Preheat oven to 325F (165C).

Remove half of mixture from dish and set aside. Arrange peaches on top of rice in dish and cover with remaining rice. Bake 25 minutes. Preheat broiler. Sprinkle pudding with remaining sugar and broil until sugar melts and turns a deep golden brown. Serve warm.

Makes 6 to 8 servings.

COFFEE BRULÉE

8 egg yolks
1/2 cup sugar
1 cup whole milk
2 cups whipping cream
1 teaspoon coffee flavoring
Summer berries, to decorate
TOPPING:
1/4 cup sugar

In a large bowl, beat together egg yolks and sugar until light and foamy.

Put milk, cream and coffee flavoring in a flameproof casserole dish. Simmer but do not boil. Remove from heat and let cool. Preheat oven to 300F (150C). Pour milk mixture into egg yolk mixture and stir well. Pour into a measuring cup and allow froth to rise to surface. Skim off froth. Pour mixture back into dish.

Put a piece of waxed paper in a roasting pan. Put dish on top of paper. Pour enough boiling water into pan to come halfway up side of dish. Bake 45 minutes or until mixture has set. Let cool slightly, then refrigerate. To make topping, preheat broiler. Sprinkle top of custard with sugar and broil until sugar melts and turns a deep golden brown. Decorate with summer berries and serve.

Makes 6 servings.

——————WINTER FRUIT SALAD——————

4 oz. dried apricots
4 oz. dried apples
4 oz. pitted prunes
1/3 cup dark raisins
1/3 cup golden raisins
1-3/4 cups unsweetened apple juice
2 (2-inch) cinnamon sticks
1 pear, peeled, cored and quartered
Thinly pared zest of 1/2 lemon

Put dried fruit, apple juice and cinnamon sticks into a flameproof casserole dish. Cover and macerate 12 hours.

Add pear and lemon zest to dish. Bring to a boil, reduce heat and simmer 15 minutes.

Remove cinnamon sticks and strips of lemon zest. Serve warm or cold.

Makes 4 to 6 servings.

SAUCY LIME PUDDING

1/4 cup unsalted butter, softened
1/4 cup sugar
Grated zest and juice of 3 limes
2 eggs, separated
1/2 cup self-rising flour
1-1/4 cups milk

Preheat oven to 325F (160C). In a large bowl, beat together butter, sugar and lime zest until light and fluffy. Stir in egg yolks and carefully fold in flour. Stir in milk and lime juice.

Whisk egg whites until they form stiff peaks. Fold into lime mixture. Lightly butter an ovenproof dish.

Pour lime mixture into dish and bake 40 to 50 minutes, or until risen and golden. Serve warm.

Makes 4 to 6 servings.

──PRUNE & ALMOND TART──

8oz. pitted prunes
1/4 cup brandy
Pie crust for 9-inch pie, thawed if frozen
1/2 cup unsalted butter, softened
1/2 cup powdered sugar
3 eggs, beaten
1/2 cup all-purpose flour
1/2 cup ground almonds
1/2 cup sliced almonds

Put prunes and brandy into a bowl and soak overnight. Roll out pastry slightly and use to line a 10-inch tart dish.

Trim pastry and prick bottom all over with a fork. Drain prunes and arrange in pastry shell. Preheat oven to 400F (205C). In a bowl, beat together butter and powdered sugar. Beat in eggs and fold in flour and ground almonds. Spread mixture evenly over prunes.

Sprinkle sliced almonds over top. Bake 40 to 45 minutes, or until filling is risen and golden brown. Serve warm.

Makes 6 to 8 servings.

QUEEN OF PUDDINGS

2-1/4 cups milk
1/4 cup butter
2 cups cake crumbs
Grated zest of 1 lemon
Grated zest of 1 orange
1/4 cup sugar
4 egg yolks, beaten
2 egg whites, beaten until stiff
1/4 cup strawberry jelly
4 oz. strawberries, sliced
Powdered sugar for dusting
MERINGUE:
2 egg whites
1/4 cup sugar

Preheat oven to 325F (165C). Put milk and butter into a flameproof casserole dish and heat gently until butter melts. Stir in cake crumbs and lemon and orange zests. Whisk in sugar and egg yolks. Fold in egg whites. Put dish in a deep roasting pan and pour in enough boiling water to come halfway up side of dish. Bake 45 to 50 minutes or until set. Mix together jelly and strawberries and spread over top of pudding.

Remove pudding from water. To make meringue, beat egg whites until they form stiff peaks. Beat in sugar. Put mixture in a pastry bag with a star tip and pipe in a lattice pattern on top of pudding. Dust with powdered sugar and bake 30 minutes. Serve warm.

Makes 4 to 6 servings.

Note: Queen of Puddings is a classic English dessert.

INDEX